peace
in everyday
relationships

Resolving Conflicts in
Your Personal and Work Life

SHEILA ALSON **&** GAYLE BURNETT

Hunter House PUBLISHERS

Hunter House Inc., Publishers
PO Box 2914
Alameda CA 94501-0914

Library of Congress Cataloging-in-Publication Data

Alson, Sheila.
Peace in everyday relationships : resolving conflicts in your personal and work life / Sheila Alson and Gayle Burnett.—1st ed.
p. cm.
Includes bibliographical references and index.
ISBN 0-89793-352-4 (pbk.) – ISBN 0-89793-353-2 (hardcover)
1. Interpersonal conflict. 2. Conflict management. I. Burnett, Gayle. II. Title.
HM1121.A47 2003
303.6'9—dc21   003012851

Project Credits

Cover Design: Brian Dittmar Graphic Design
Book Production: Hunter House
Developmental & Copy Editor: Kelley Blewster
Proofreader: Lee Rappold
Indexer: Nancy D. Peterson
Acquisitions Editor: Jeanne Brondino
Editor: Alexandra Mummery
Publicist: Lisa E. Lee
Foreign Rights Assistant: Elisabeth Wohofsky
Customer Service Manager: Christina Sverdrup
Order Fulfillment: Lakdhon Lama
Administrator: Theresa Nelson
Computer Support: Peter Eichelberger
Publisher: Kiran S. Rana

Manufactured in Canada by Transcontinental Printing

9 8 7 6 5 4 3 2 1   First Edition   03 04 05 06 07

Peace in Everyday Relationships

DEDICATION

To my children, Rebecca and Jesse Alson-Milkman

— SHEILA ALSON

For Jasmine-Sky Burnett and the world she creates

— GAYLE BURNETT

Ordering

Trade bookstores in the U.S. and Canada please contact:

Publishers Group West
1700 Fourth Street, Berkeley CA 94710
Phone: (800) 788-3123   Fax: (510) 528-3444

Hunter House books are available at bulk discounts for textbook course adoptions; to qualifying community, health-care, and government organizations; and for special promotions and fund-raising. For details please contact:

Special Sales Department
Hunter House Inc., PO Box 2914, Alameda CA 94501-0914
Phone: (510) 865-5282   Fax: (510) 865-4295
E-mail: sales@hunterhouse.com

Individuals can order our books from most bookstores, by calling **(800) 266-5592,** or from our website at **www.hunterhouse.com**

Contents

Important Note

The material in this book is intended to provide a review of information regarding conflict resolution, communication, and emotional intelligence. Every effort has been made to provide accurate and dependable information. The contents of this book have been compiled through professional research and in consultation with mental-health professionals. However, professionals in the field have differing opinions, and change is always taking place.

Therefore, the publisher, authors, and editors, and the professionals quoted in the book cannot be held responsible for any error, omission, or dated material. The authors and publisher assume no responsibility for any outcome of applying the information in this book in a program of self-care or under the care of a licensed practitioner. If you have questions concerning your relationships, or about the application of the information described in this book, consult a qualified mental-health professional.

Preface

I write this seven months after 11 September 2001, a day when thousands lost their lives over an unresolved conflict that has plagued our planet for thousands of years. In the past year, since I began to write this book, my own life has been invaded by intense interpersonal conflict. Most of us long for peace. We remember to include a wish for peace in our holiday prayers and in our mindful daily meditations. Yet it often remains a longing, a distant possibility that seems out of our reach. How do we get there, to a place and time when we live peacefully with one another?

Our tendency is to want simple instructions for life. Books about how to improve our lives abound, each prescribing a few easy steps to follow in order to resolve conflicts, achieve success, find love, create wealth, and more. However, my life does not allow me to say to you, the readers, that creating peace in our relationships is easy.

I have been in the field of conflict resolution for seventeen years as a trainer and a mediator. I have studied conflict resolution in both formal and informal settings and have trained many people, preschool children through senior adults, in how to resolve their conflicts. I have mediated hundreds of family, relationship, workplace, schoolyard, and neighborhood conflicts. I have applied the skills and concepts of conflict resolution to my own life whenever I could. In the spirit of telling the truth, I need to say that it works—most of the time. However, there are situations that remain baffling and intractable, on both a personal and global level. There are conflicts that continue to rage in spite of the best efforts of peacemakers.

So, is there hope?

Just as my life has sent me challenges, it has also sent me messages of hope and of peace. Forces of destruction may take hold of us sometimes, but forces of healing also exist. Intention is everything.

If we can summon the intention in our lives to create peace, and maintain that intention, even in the face of war and destruction, then peace will be created.

This book contains useful tools—information, approaches, concepts, and skills—that you can apply to your life's journey. These tools will aid you in your intention to create peace, and will help you remain steadfast when challenges arise. The tools, however, are not magic. The magic lies in your mindfulness and your attention to the intangible connection among all human beings on the planet. The magic lies in your intention and your desire to stay true to the goal of creating peace, even in the face of difficulty and in the midst of hurt, fear, envy, jealousy, anger, or desire for revenge. Creating peace is a lifelong journey. You would not be reading this book unless you had the desire to embark on such a journey.

My life has been a laboratory where I've forged the knowledge base that informs this book. In the same way, the lives of my clients, neighbors, friends, family members, and coworkers have all contributed to the concepts espoused in this book. The conclusions I draw are based on a combination of research in the field and data from my own experience and the experience of my clients and students. All of our lives teach us valuable lessons if we are open and willing to learn.

I invite you to join the growing number of people whose intention is to create peace both for their own lives and for the planet as a whole.

— SHEILA ALSON
24 APRIL 2002

Less than a month after writing the Preface, Sheila was diagnosed with a life-threatening illness that would eventually take its toll. Since we worked together in a wide variety of venues, as consultants, mediators, and coaches in the fields of diversity and conflict resolution, and because we developed a friendship and kinship through that work, she asked me to complete her work on this book. I, for my part, have lovingly done my best. Whatever brilliance or insight you find within these pages, freely attribute them to Sheila. Should there be errors, omissions, or failures, I gladly count them as mine.

Sheila was a courageous woman whose dedication to peace is an example to those of us who continue the work. I am honored to be a part of this project, and I thank you, the reader, for joining us on this journey.

— GAYLE BURNETT
27 NOVEMBER 2002

Acknowledgments

First I would like to thank my teachers. I began in the field of conflict resolution in 1985 when Tom Roderick, executive director of Educators for Social Responsibility, Metropolitan Area, came into a class I was teaching at PS 321, in Brooklyn. Tom and his colleague Linda Lantieri introduced me to the skills and concepts of conflict resolution as they applied to conflicts in schools. Together they founded the Resolving Conflict Creatively Program, a collaboration between Educators for Social Responsibility, Metro, and the New York City Board of Education. They became my teachers for many years. I am grateful for their contribution.

I have had the privilege to work with and learn from many pioneers in the field of conflict resolution in education, including Priscilla Prutzman, of Children's Creative Response to Conflict, and Bill Kreidler, of Educators for Social Responsibility. When I branched into the field of conflict resolution and mediation for adults, I was fortunate to study with Ellen Raider, director of training at the International Center for Cooperation and Conflict Resolution at Columbia University. My work with Inter-Change Consultants introduced me to many valuable concepts and skills in the area of diversity and culture. I am grateful for the lessons I learned from the Inter-Change Partners: Gayle Burnett, Bruce Gill, Phyllis Haynes, and Elizabeth Young.

I would also like to thank the many colleagues who were all valuable teachers for me, especially Jinnie Spiegler, Ted Welch, Betsy Sason, Zephryn Conte, Mariana Gaston, Ellen Icolari, James Tobin, Manny Verdi, Wendy Constantine, and Sherrie Gammage.

I would like to thank the people who gave me encouragement and support to write this book: Carolyn Holbrook, David Henderson, and my agent, Scott Edelstein. I would like to thank those who made my life possible during the year I wrote this book: Rebecca and Jesse Alson-Milkman, Dave Bartholemew, Jr., Chandra McCormick, and Keith Calhoun.

— SHEILA ALSON

I would like to acknowledge my partners in business and in life. Elizabeth Young, Bruce Gill, and Phyllis Haynes (a.k.a. Inter-Change Consultants) have created a richness of knowledge and experience for which I can never adequately or accurately thank them. The organizations and individuals we have taught and touched have provided the living laboratory through which most of our work has been developed. I thank those organizations and individuals for allowing us to contribute to their leadership and diversity evolution.

To my colleagues and teachers, Ted Welch, Carolyn Hart, Zephryn Conti, Sherrie Grammage, Kim Jones, and Casssandra Bond: you have been the folks who immersed me in the work. You held my hands, gave advice, and guided me along the day-to-day journey of learning and sharing the ways of conflict resolution and peace.

I would also like to thank Tom Roderick, executive director of Educators for Social Responsibility, Metropolitan Area, and Linda Lantieri, cofounders of the Resolving Conflict Creatively Program. They gave me my first assignments in the field of conflict resolution, providing me with a rich grounding in the skills and language of peace.

With love beyond all understanding I honor Gloria Burnett, my mom, and Jasmine-Sky Gregory Burnett, my daughter, who have helped me hone my peace skills by providing countless situations within which to use those skills (smile). We create a home and a life, together. Thank you—without your patience and support my contribution to this book could not have been possible. An enormous thank you to the folks who kept me sane: Leda Tatum, Neasie Lundy, Michael Amos, Eric and Ethel Burnett, and the Hillside Chapel and Truth Center.

Gratitude abounds for all the folks at Hunter House, especially Kelley Blewster ("So that's what an editor does!") and Jeanne Brondino, for her willingness to keep this project going.

— GAYLE BURNETT

Introduction

ℬ

Whenever, wherever, and however people interact there are guaranteed to be opportunities for peace. Far too often, those opportunities are missed or ignored, resulting in escalated or festering conflicts. As individuals, we see and experience the world uniquely. No two of us feel or believe identically about anything or anyone, yet each of us wants to be understood and accepted by others. A lack of understanding of the differing experiences, emotional responses, and perceptions among us often causes actions and reactions that lead us away from peaceful resolution.

Sheila Alson and I bring to this book our unique perspectives on developing peaceful resolutions. During the seventeen years preceding her death, Sheila trained staff and students in conflict resolution within the New York City Public Schools, the New Orleans Public Schools, and the Anchorage Public Schools. She also worked as a psychotherapist in private practice for over ten years.

I am a partner with the international consulting firm Inter-Change Consultants. For the past fourteen years, through Inter-Change, I have consulted with numerous corporations, not-for-profit organizations, and public school systems in the areas of conflict resolution, diversity, and leadership development. When asked to join Sheila in the writing of this book, I leapt at the chance to share with readers the fundamentals of creating peaceful and rewarding relationships.

My journey into the work of conflict resolution began in third grade when my family moved to a new neighborhood. I rode a school bus every day, and because I was new I was picked on. During that first year, several children continually tormented me by pulling my hair, hitting me, and destroying my books and materials. I did not know how to respond to them. This happened during the civil rights movement, and I believed in the nonviolent message of Dr. Martin Luther King. But I had no skills that would help me stand up for myself. Their behavior continued until one day, fearing they were really going to hurt me, I punched the leader of the group in the stomach, leaving her badly shaken and gasping for air.

Although I was loudly cheered by many of my fellow bus riders, I was ashamed of the violent way I responded. I knew there had to be a better way, and my life and work have helped me find it. In this book I share what I've discovered and learned along the way, so that you can experience the power and sense of satisfaction that come from creating peace.

ℱℬ ℱℬ

One of our deepest desires as human beings is to live in harmony with one another. Each of the world's major religions supports the idea of peace, and we have created huge institutions dedicated to helping us achieve peace, such as the United Nations and the Peace Corps. We spend millions of dollars each year in an attempt to bring more harmony into our lives. From *feng shui* to the Dr. Phil phenomenon, we are searching for a way to be at peace within ourselves and with others.

The difficulty lies in our competing desires to have our basic human needs met. We each have a host of strategies to employ if it appears that some need will go unfulfilled. Most of these strategies we learned while growing up, or when embarking upon a journey into new territory, like starting a first job. We look to those around us, those who know the terrain, to show us the way. Unfortunately, many individuals whom we learn from received their training in the ways to "win" a conflict (no matter how bloody the battlefield)—rather than in how to create peaceful resolution.

A huge difference exists between "winning" and creating peaceful resolution. We'll explore that later in the book. For now it's enough to understand that if any one of us leaves a conflict feeling wounded or as if we're powerless, the conflict is not resolved—it's temporarily tabled.

Much of today's business practices, though often using the terminology of resolution, are really focused on overpowering and besting someone else. The workplaces where we spend the bulk of our days are highly competitive and stressful. We work at being smarter, faster, and better networked than the next person, in the hopes that we will win out in the end. These may be potentially good strategies for dealing with our common business tasks, but they rarely work when trying to deal with human beings.

I have a wonderful friend whose primary strategy for dealing with difficulties in her romantic relationships is to end them. As you might imagine, she has ended a couple of marriages and several serious relationships this way. When she got married the last time, three years ago, she told me, "This one is going to stick; he's a good man and we love each other."

A year later she called me to say that she had the phone book open and was looking for a mover. As she began to punch in the first numbers, it occurred to her that she was about to repeat a scene in her life that she seemed to re-create over and over again. At that moment, she decided that maybe *she* had some changing to do. She and I have spent many hours since that call reflecting on her needs, the way she expresses them, and the possible alternative skills she can use to get her needs met.

Peace in Everyday Relationships: Resolving Conflicts in Your Personal and Work Life will provide you with a new and focused way of dealing with the people around you. We'll explore the skills you need in order to be more successful in your relationships with others—from family and friends to colleagues and bosses. Sheila and I give examples from our own lives and from our consulting practices. You'll read of our successes, mistakes, and missteps. We will share with you the journey we have undertaken to create peace in our world.

You may want to begin a peacework journal. Throughout the book are exercises and activities. Use the journal to write down your responses to our questions; use it also to record any reflections about conflict that arise as you read. Much of the work of learning peace skills will require that you begin to see the patterns of behavior that keep you from creating peace. A journal is very helpful in this process, because you can return to it to reflect on similarities and differences in your behavior over time.

Peaceful resolution requires that we reframe the entire way we look at and respond to conflict. It necessitates that we fully understand our own needs in a conflict, and that we act not out of anger or fear, but rather out of the possibility of fruitful and creative problem solving. In order to create a lasting peace out of conflict, we must join with those with whom we are having difficulty and seek out a solution to our problem. That solution must then meet the needs of all involved, so that each of us walks away satisfied.

Many of you may be coming to this book thinking we will teach you how to change yourself or your loved ones so that you don't have conflicts. While using the skills in this book will certainly reduce the number and intensity of the conflicts you may have, as Sheila said in the Preface, there is no magic formula that will take away your conflicts. However, reading this book is taking a step toward change. It's a step toward changing the way you handle one of the most common and complex aspects of your life—conflict.

Creating peace is a process. It is far richer than the elimination of discord. It is the ability to experience conflict without losing yourself. First, however, you have to know yourself. In this book we will ask you to look very closely at yourself and the way you handle conflict. You will be asked to reflect on how you currently deal with conflicts, to learn and practice the skills of peaceful resolution, and then to use them in conflict situations. Exercises are presented at the end of major chapters that are designed to help you use the information provided. Many of the skills we discuss will take practice before they feel natural. So take the time to read and use these exercises. They will help you become more comfortable with the skills of peaceful resolution and make it easier for you to choose to use them when you are in a conflict.

On 10 December 2001, Kofi A. Annan, Nobel Peace Prize Laureate, said the following in his lecture before the Norwegian Nobel Committee:

> In this new century, we must start from the understanding that peace belongs not only to states or peoples, but to each and every member of those communities.... Peace must be made real and tangible in the daily existence of every individual in need. Peace must be sought, above all, because it is the condition for every member of the human family to live a life of dignity and security.

If peace is to be achieved, it will require individual effort in our daily lives, as much as it will require global diplomatic attention. Creating peace in your everyday relationships will mean becoming different by taking on the challenge to relate to friends, family, coworkers, and strangers in a new way. This book is meant to guide and help you along the way.

There is a wonderful song that opens with the lines "Let there be peace on earth, and let it begin with me." Begin with yourself today, and stay the course, because peace is created one human interaction at a time.

— GAYLE BURNETT

Part I

❦❦

Changing the Way We Fight

CHAPTER 1

ℰ

Resolving Conflict Peacefully Is a Choice

Gerald and Susan are getting a divorce. They have been referred by a family-counseling agency to Sheila, a trained mediator. As their mediator, Sheila will act as an impartial party to guide them through the dangerous waters of blame and anger, helping them to hear and better understand one another.

At this point, the list of mutual atrocities between Susan and Gerald is so long that every time they try to explain why they can no longer be together they have another painful story to tell. The latest story goes like this: she says he humiliated her in front of her friends by ridiculing her about the dinner she made, and he always does that. He says she bought a new dress for herself when they didn't even have enough money to meet their bills this month, and she's never careful about money. She says he'll spend money on taking a cab instead of the subway, while she has to drag two children and a stroller on the bus every morning to child care. He says she deliberately cooks food that he has trouble digesting just to show off for her friends. She says he didn't lift a finger to help cook the meal. He says she didn't even consult with him about whether he wanted to spend an evening with those people. And the accusations go on and on and on.

Susan and Gerald are not bad people. They are caught in a cycle of conflict, and they are very unhappy. One conflict leads to another, and soon they are hurling insults at each other. To take a break from insults, sometimes they just stay away from each other. There are weeks at a time when their conversations consist solely of "Please pass the salt," "Can you pick up the kids from day care today?" and other necessities.

The only way they see out of the situation is to get a divorce, but they have two children to whom they are both committed. And even after the divorce, it's likely that they will spend the rest of their lives playing out this cycle with each other over the children. Maybe it will be over money or custody or visitation or who gets to have the kids on Thanksgiving.

How did they get to this point with each other? Wasn't there a time when being together was the right choice? Why is everything so difficult?

Conflict that feels intractable is just as common in the workplace as it is in the home. Melanie has been working at the same job for over twelve years and has received the requisite increases in pay, but she feels that her hard work is continually overlooked and underrewarded. She is still working in a little cubicle that affords her no privacy, no space, and no amenities. A small office has been vacant on the floor for months, and she is the most senior person in her job classification. She requested the office months ago, but has gotten no response from her boss, Ray. Her boss is okay, but Melanie feels he doesn't go to bat for her. He thinks only of his own career.

There is no way Melanie can leave the job. She's put in a lot of time and has built up a good pension. She has a family to support. But it no longer makes sense to her to work as hard as she does. She's thinking she might as well just put in the minimum every day and go home.

Actually, Ray, Melanie's boss, has been going to bat for her for months within the department's management team. He's trying to get her not only the office but a promotion as well. He's taking a lot of heat for it. The promotion and the vacant office have become political footballs on the management team.

The primary opposition to Melanie's promotion is coming from Becky, who wants to hold up promotions until the department has standardized its promotion criteria. Becky feels that standardized criteria are important in order to combat favoritism, the "old boy" network that has existed in the company from time immemorial.

This is a complex web of conflict. If the people involved can't find their way out of it, resentments will fester, blame will be passed around, work will suffer, and the productivity of the department will decrease.

John prefers the heat on high; Melissa likes to keep the room cooler. Carol wants to do the dishes later, and her dad wants them cleaned up now. Walter wants to get out of the family gathering his mother planned, but his mother keeps insisting that he come. Mark's tailor wants to keep his jacket for a week for alterations, but Mark needs it back by Friday. One of Nancy's friends likes to call her long distance after 11:00 P.M., and Nancy likes to sleep.

Conflict Is Everywhere

To be human is to engage in conflict. Whether it occurs at home, at work, or in our social lives, conflict is here to stay. Acknowledging this reality leaves us with a choice: We can effectively handle conflict or not. When we choose to effectively handle conflict we are opening ourselves up to many possibilities. We may discover that we lacked some of the information we needed, that our assumptions were incorrect, or that we were focusing on the past instead of the present. Or we may find that we were absolutely right in our understanding of the situation and of the other person—but that's a less likely outcome.

By contrast, when we choose to react to conflict in the same old ways we always have, we risk doing more damage to our relationships by assigning blame and limiting our opportunities to understand other points of view. Most of us engage in conflict with the idea that we are right and we will win. But the complexity of human beings means that there is more gray than black and white.

Conflict may drive us crazy, but it also drives us to creation. Handled well, conflict has the potential to propel us forward, to point the way to a fresh understanding, to help us discover something new in the process of resolution. Sometimes, however, in the midst of our conflicts it is hard to find a way to create anything but regret.

As an inevitable part of life, conflict is neither good nor bad. It is as simple as a disagreement, and since it is impossible to agree with everyone all the time, conflict will always be with us.

Most of the conflicts we encounter are easily dealt with. The strategies we have already developed are perfectly adequate to help us navigate through minor frustrations. We developed these methods through trial and error, from messages about conflict we got as we were growing up, and from hints we picked up along the way. Many of these strategies are connected to the emotions we felt during past conflicts that we either witnessed or experienced. When the emotions arise, our strategies for how to deal with the situation are summoned.

In the face of strong and difficult emotions like anger, rage, despair, frustration, and fear, adrenaline is pumped into our system to make us strong, causing our heart rate to increase. We grow hot. Our face becomes flushed. Blood is pumped out of the digestive system and into the limbs, preparing us to either fight or run away. Our stomach becomes tight. Our neck stiffens. This physiological response has been called the *fight-or-flight response*. It is an evolutionary survival mechanism that remains imprinted in our brain. Accompanying these signals are mental messages that tell us which strategy to employ so we can successfully attack or escape. We may curse, scream, accuse, ridicule, or devise means of revenge. We may leave the scene, cease talking, create excuses for avoiding the conflict altogether, or physically attack.

Most of us rarely if ever find ourselves in the life-threatening situations from which this physiological response was designed to protect us. Still, the emotions that trigger the response are all too common, and if we had a Richter scale for feelings, we would see that we each have a different tolerance level for the rumblings of our emotions. In some it takes a large dose of anger to trigger the physiological reactions involved in the fight-or-flight response. In others, there is little space between frustration and rage, little time between calm and chaos. But there is a point for all of us when the adrenaline reaction that signals fight or flight is set off. In Chapter 2 we'll take a closer look at the fight-or-flight response and the impact it has on creating resolution.

A Desire for Peace

In spite of our physiologically driven fight-or-flight response, our deepest desire in conflict is to return to peace. This desire for peace is expressed in many ways. Over three hundred prizes for peace are currently awarded worldwide, in addition to the Nobel Peace Prize. A simple search on the Barnes and Noble website using the keywords *peace* and *self-help* returns a list of 835 in-print books. A search on the site with only the keyword *peace* supplies 5,791 current titles. We are a culture literally searching for peace, in our personal lives and in the world at large, and we are not alone. The European University Center for Peace Studies, the Peace Corps, the Millennium World Peace Summit, Australia's World Peace Bell (constructed from coins donated from around the world), the Dalai Lama, Nelson Mandela, Gandhi, Martin Luther King, Jr., and the inexhaustible list of other symbols, heroes, and institutions large and small that are dedicated to the creation of peace are all proof of our desire for peaceful coexistence.

Yet when we look at our world today, and when we review history, we see a great deal of conflict and violence. War, terrorism, and cynicism threaten us as much today as they ever have. In our day-to-day lives we are confronted with violence in our schools, at work, and, for too many of us, in our homes. So, if there is so much violence taking place so much of the time, who is it that wants peace?

We all do, on some level. But like everything else, the violence we see around us is a result of the way we see the world. When we view the world as hostile and threatening, we will make choices that protect us from those threats. We will strike out with our words or fists, hurting others because or before we ourselves have been hurt. But these confrontations often leave us feeling shaken, even if we "win" the battle. And without a resolution that satisfies the needs of all involved, the war will continue.

Creating peace doesn't mean that we ignore our problems. It doesn't mean that we pretend nothing is going on in order to avoid a battle. In fact, the opposite is true. In order to have peace, we must be open and clear about when our needs are not being met. More than that, and often much more challenging, we must be willing to discover the needs of the others involved in the conflict, and then find solutions that meet those needs. Resolving conflict is a far more complex process than simply overpowering an opponent with words, strategy, or physical prowess.

Why is there so much violence in the world if we all crave peace? We believe it is because most people lack the skills needed for achieving peace. Everybody wants it, but most of us don't know how to get it. Many of us keep using the strategies that lead to separation or violence because they are all we know. But as a wise person once said, "If you keep doing what you've always done, you'll just keep getting the same old thing." In other words, old ways of thinking about conflict can't lead to new ways of creating peace.

Our popular television soap operas, reality shows, and talk shows all provide us with glimpses into how most people handle conflict. From the explicit destroy-or-be-destroyed tactics used on reality TV, to the manipulative strategies and mindsets reflected in the soaps, we learn to coerce, cajole, intimidate, lie, build alliances designed to eliminate others, pretend to be who we are not, and engage in a host of other behaviors that work against resolution.

All around us, behaviors are portrayed that encourage lingering and escalating conflict, and mindsets are explored that utilize such tactics. But there is little exploration of strategies that heal and bring satisfaction out of conflict.

Popular psychology tells us that we are addicted to drama. It's little wonder we absorb this message when we continue to portray the world around us in such negatively dramatic ways. While the media reflects our addiction to drama, it also feeds and reinforces that addiction. Our children watch us use the strategies portrayed on our favorite television shows, hear us discuss with excitement the losses of others, and learn the same rules we learned for how to handle conflict ineffectively and with little concern for the others involved.

When the Los Angeles riots broke out after the acquittal of the police officers who beat Rodney King, Mr. King echoed the heartfelt plea of many Americans: "Can't we all just get along?" The answer is yes. But first we have to learn how.

The first step in learning how to create peace is to understand the cycle of conflict. We need to know how conflict works in order to develop effective strategies for resolving it. The chapter's next section breaks down the component parts of the conflict cycle so that we can take a close look at each one.

The Conflict Cycle

Conflicts progress along a series of steps that can more or less be predicted. These steps include a cause, an incident, a response, and an outcome. Together these steps are referred to as the *conflict cycle*. Let's examine the conflict cycle as exemplified by a disagreement between Julie and her mother, Rose.

Rose wanted Julie to attend a family gathering. It was scheduled for April 3, and Julie was buried in a mountain of tax paperwork, so she called Rose and said she couldn't go. Her mom said, "You're always so busy. You never seem to have time for family."

Julie said, "Give me a break, Mom. Try not to lay on the guilt too thick. I have to do my taxes. I have no choice."

Rose said, "Hmm."

Julie said, "Hmm."

Rose said, "Okay, fine, but I'll remember this."

Julie said, "Good."

They hung up.

Then a little voice inside Julie said, "You should be good to your mother. She's getting older and you need to spend time with her now." So she made the choice to appease her mother, called her back, and said she would go. But this wasn't a choice made to resolve the conflict; it was a choice made to avoid feeling guilty.

This was just one incident in their continuing cycle of conflict over spending time together. The *cause* of a conflict is a perceived incompatibility of desires. Rose says she wants Julie to spend more time with her. Julie says she wants and needs to spend the time in other pursuits. There are times when these desires seem incompatible and a conflict ensues.

In the incident above, time was very tight (the *cause*). It was a scarce commodity. When Rose raised the issue about where Julie would be on Sunday (the *incident*), conflict ensued because it seemed that Rose's desire for Julie's attendance and Julie's desire to do her taxes were not compatible. Their *responses* to the conflict were very similar in foundation. Rose guilt-tripped Julie. Julie attacked Rose. Both were hostile fight responses. Julie eventually gave in. The *outcome* was that Rose got her way this time, and Julie didn't.

However, Julie harbored resentment toward Rose as a result. An outcome to a conflict that doesn't leave both people feeling satisfied generally contributes to causing the next conflict. Thus, conflict recycles. That's exactly what happened in Julie and Rose's case. Julie was present at the gathering, but she definitely wasn't warm and friendly to her mother. Rose picked up on Julie's attitude, and this led to yet another conflict.

If you look closely at the cycle these two women were caught in, you can see that there were a number of points along the way where a different choice made by either of them could have changed the course of the conflict and led to a peaceful resolution.

The rest of this chapter discusses *mindset*: how we view a conflict and how that view often leads to destructive responses (choices) and unsatisfactory outcomes. If we fail to clearly see our conflicts and their possible outcomes, we cannot make choices that lead to peaceful resolutions. In the scenario above, either Julie or Rose might have made the choice to express more of the feelings behind their words. Julie might have explained that she wanted to see Rose, but that this was the time of year when she was under a great deal of stress. She might have said that she would come and spend the day with Rose right after tax time. Rose might have expressed that she missed Julie, and that she loves her and knows how hard she is working. In fact, Rose is worried about how hard Julie is working, and wants her to take a break. These are just a couple of the missed opportunities they could have chosen from if either had adopted a mindset of understanding and being under-stood.

Part of productively dealing with conflict means acquiring a different mindset about possibilities. Part of the shift to a different mindset involves acquiring skill in handling difficult situations.

Outcomes: The Shift Toward Possibilities

In the conflict about the family gathering, the outcome was that Rose "won" and Julie "lost": Julie went to the gathering. However, the tax forms she needed to prepare failed to get done, and she had to stay up late the following night to finish them in time. Although she told herself it was okay to put herself out for a little while to please her mother, Julie was feeling less generous at three in the morning. Rose eventually heard about it from Julie; a little anger and guilt were directed her way the next opportunity Julie got. In the end, neither of them experienced much peace.

However, had the conflict ended the opposite way, with Rose losing and Julie winning, Rose would have resented her daughter for skipping the gathering and probably would have found a way to retaliate. Again, the conflict would have recycled, and the opportunity for peace would have been lost.

In conflict, winning has a different meaning than it does in a game. In conflict, winning is not about scoring more points, but about feeling satisfied.

Many years ago, when Sheila's children were small, they often fought over which TV show to watch. Sometimes the fight would escalate and the noise level in the living room would increase. Eventually, Sheila would stomp into the living room, shut off the TV, and say, "Nobody watches." At the time Sheila thought this was a good solution, but in fact it made both of her children losers in the TV war. Was this fair? Well, it was certainly equal since neither got what they wanted, but what was the real result? They both continued to resent each other, and the TV conflict grew more bitter next time. It was a *lose-lose outcome*. Though Sheila brought quiet to the living room for the moment, quiet does not always mean peace. Both of her children were silently plotting revenge.

We are at peace when we are satisfied. However, if we are satisfied and the other person is not, we won't be satisfied for long. The other person will see to it that we are not. We return to peace only if we can both walk away feeling satisfied. When this happens, it's called a *win-win solution*. This is a foundational concept, and we'll build on the mindset of win-win, of creating solutions that allow both parties to win, throughout this chapter.

So, if Rose wanted Julie to come to the gathering, and Julie wanted to skip it, how could they both have gotten what they wanted?

Rose and Julie were looking at this conflict as a competition in which only one of them was going to get her way. They looked at the conflict in terms of win-lose outcomes. Either Julie went to the gathering, or Julie stayed home.

The first mental shift they could have made involves understanding that in most conflict situations many outcomes are possible—not just the obvious, polarized positions. Instead of competing to win, they could have made the choice to cooperate with each other and begun the search for a win-win solution. They could have become partners in the search for satisfaction, helping themselves and one another along the way. (We'll talk more about how to engage the other person as a partner in Part III.)

Causes: Positions Versus Needs

Generally, when a conflict begins, the conflict is framed around what we want. Rose wanted Julie to go to the gathering. Julie wanted to stay home and do her taxes. These expressions of what they wanted were their *positions*. If the positions initially seem incompatible, a little more digging can reveal new possibilities.

We may initially think that getting what we say we want is the only way to reach satisfaction. However, if we ask the other person, "Why do you want that?" and if we ask ourselves, "Why do I want what I want?" we may discover what underlies those positions— which is what each person truly *needs*. Our *position* is how we initially think we can satisfy our needs. But the overarching condition to resolving the conflict is getting our needs met. And many ways may exist to meet those needs.

Rose's underlying need was to feel the sense of belonging and love she got when her family was together. Julie's underlying need was to maintain the security of her own family by completing her taxes on time. Each woman also had the need to be respected by the other. Needs can be tangible, such as time and money. They can also be psychological, such as belonging, love, and respect. Here are some examples of these different needs.

Tangible Needs

Food	Clothing	Shelter
Water	Sex	Health
Money	Time	Rest
Job	Raise in pay	Space
Tools	Vacation	Sick days
Telephone	Transportation	Physical safety
Clean environment		Crime-free environment
Access to entertainment		A certain level of education

Psychological Needs

Love	Affection	Emotional safety
Self-esteem	Belonging	Recognition
Respect	Fun	Growth
Fulfillment	Freedom	Independence
Courage	Power	Hope
Affiliation	Status	Praise
Learning	Self-actualization	
Equality	Pleasure	

Meeting Needs: Reframing the Conflict

Once we have recognized what each person's underlying needs might be, then all sorts of alternatives begin to emerge for meeting those needs.

In the case of psychological needs, a profound shift occurs when we realize that the intangibles that fulfill those needs are unlimited, not scarce. It's not as if there are small pots of treasure labeled "respect," "appreciation," and "love" that must be divided. These gifts are potentially in infinite supply in the world. Fine, but what does this have to do with resolving conflict? Well, if respect is an underlying need in a conflict, for example, then it is possible even in the midst of conflict to find opportunities for both people to provide respect for the other. Sometimes the act of giving respect can be demonstrated in the very manner in which we talk to each other while we are angry. Likewise, appreciation can come from the way people are listened to while they are trying to express themselves.

Often both tangible and psychological needs underlie a conflict, but we are not always aware of our psychological needs. It's common to fight fiercely on the battleground of tangible needs, when the real issue is a hidden psychological need. Sometimes simply asking ourselves why we want a particular tangible need can help bring our psychological need to the surface. You'll have a chance to practice finding your underlying tangible and psychological needs in the exercise at the end of the chapter.

Let's look again at the conflict between Rose and Julie, and try to perceive it in a new way—that is, try to *reframe* it. If Rose could come to feel a sense of belonging and love, and Julie could maintain the security of her family, then they would both end up feeling satisfied. By realizing this, we have reframed the conflict around needs rather than positions.

Here are some ways the two women could have acknowledged Rose's need for belonging and provided other opportunities for her to feel her family's love without interfering with Julie's need for security:

1. Rose could move the gathering to another day.

2. Julie and Rose could schedule a separate get-together after Julie's taxes are done.

If the gathering remained on the same day and Julie agreed to come, Rose could compensate for that concession in any of the following ways:

1. Julie could file for an extension of the deadline to pay taxes, and then finish them after the gathering. To offset this inconvenience, Rose could offer to watch Julie's kids for an afternoon.

2. Rose could offer Julie seventy dollars to pay for ten hours of babysitting. While the sitter watched her kids, Julie could finish her taxes and have enough time left over to go to the family gathering.

3. Julie could bring some of the paperwork to Rose's house before the gathering, and Rose could help Julie with some of the tasks.

4. Rose (who is a bookkeeper) could do a considerable amount of Julie's tax preparation herself after the gathering.

In order for a solution to be considered win-win, both parties must feel that it genuinely meets their needs. What Julie may think is a win for Rose may not really meet Rose's needs, and vice versa. Mother and daughter, therefore, have to explore their needs together and create as many alternative solutions as they can that will make them both happy. Reframing the conflict—from a competition for positions to a cooperative effort to get both parties' needs met—opens up a number of solutions that can bring people to peace.

Because our desire is to return to peace, choosing to deal constructively with conflict is one of the crucial elements for a fulfilling and satisfying life. Understanding the basics of conflict—its cycles and frames—helps in our quest for peaceful relationships. The first step toward a greater insight into the discord in our lives is realizing that much of what we see as conflict stems from *the way* we see it. Too often, conflict is viewed as competition. In other words, there is always a loser. Taking this approach leads to a continuous cycle of disagreement, examples of which abound—from petty squabbles between coworkers to the intractable violence among nations. By shifting our view of conflict away from the competition model, new possibilities for cooperation open to us. After all, we are all in conflict together.

We move now from the basic elements of conflict to some of its root causes. In the next chapter, we will dig deeper into the ways in which conflict affects us—both physically and psychologically—and, in turn, the ways we affect the conflicts in our lives.

℘ Exercise: Identifying Needs

Have paper and pen handy, or write in your peacework journal.

1. Think back to a recent, fairly minor conflict you experienced with a family member, spouse or life partner, coworker, friend, acquaintance, or even stranger (such as a store clerk or customer service representative). Try to select a conflict that still makes you feel angry or anxious when you think about it.

2. Write down what your *position* was—that is, what you seemed to want during the conflict.

3. Write down what the other person's position was, as you understand it. Hold on to this information for later. We will return to considering the other person in Chapter 4.

4. Now close your eyes, take a few deep, calming breaths, and ask yourself, "*Why* did I want what I wanted in that conflict?" Chances are, several answers will come to mind. Write down whatever pops up. Don't edit yourself; just write.

5. Looking at what you have written, select the one or two responses that cause the strongest feeling for you and ask yourself, "Why is that important?" For example, about a conflict with a waiter who brought you the wrong food order, you might have written, "My need is to have the food I asked for brought to me since I'm paying for it," and "I needed to finish lunch by 1:00 because of a 1:30 meeting with an important potential client." The need with the most charge is probably related to the 1:30 meeting. When you ask yourself why it is important, concerns about money might surface. This concern may be connected to a psychological need for freedom to live a particular lifestyle and to the tangible needs for food, clothing, and shelter.

6. Distill what you wrote down in step 5 into *underlying needs* as expressed in one or two words each. If you wish, review the lists of tangible and psychological needs on pages 18–19 to help you come up with words that suitably express your needs. Again, you will likely have more than one answer.

In the exercise accompanying Chapter 4 we will brainstorm ways to come up with win-win solutions to this conflict.

CHAPTER 2

ℯ𝒶

Identifying
What Triggers Conflict

Another pair of Sheila's clients, Michael and his wife, Ellen, are continually at war with each other. Michael is particularly adept at using words in discussion, Ellen is less so. His goal is to prove that his position is right and Ellen's position is wrong. In contrast, Ellen's style is to withdraw. Their most recent struggle is about where to live. They currently live in New York City. Michael wants to remain in New York. Ellen wants to move to the country. They have rented a small country house that they visit every other weekend, but Ellen feels this is not enough. Even though each has given up a little of what he or she wants, the arrangement doesn't meet either of their underlying needs.

They both have a good sense of what the other person's need is. Michael is a writer and is very active in the New York arts communities. He wants to continue to attend literary events, go to art galleries, and so on. His need is for stimulation, excitement, and career advancement. Ellen is an herbalist who has studied the subject for many years. She gets a lot of satisfaction from taking long walks in the woods and gathering wild herbs, which she dries and makes into teas and tinctures. She likes solitude and natural surroundings. Her need is for self-fulfillment and inner peace. They have a child who is about to start kindergarten, and despite years of conflict, they are still devoted to each other and to the family they have created.

Michael has tried often to convince Ellen of the merits of the city, and to weaken her position by pointing out the qualities of the country he finds objectionable. Ellen does not bring up arguments to support her position but reacts to Michael's arguments with silence. She has developed this style after many years of living with Michael and losing her arguments with him; she avoids the arguments altogether by refusing to engage in them. This drives Michael crazy. He wants her to state her position and do battle. He wants her to say what she wants, but instead she grows quiet and becomes sad.

One day, he begins to ridicule her: "Say something, Ellen! It's b——-s—- the way you just sit there, like an ugly lump."

She answers, "Why do you talk like that?"

"Why don't you answer me, why don't you say something to let me know you're alive?"

She grows silent again and leaves the room.

The next morning Ellen says to Michael, "I'm taking Jasmine and enrolling her in a school in the country. We're moving. I hope you'll come to see us two weekends a month. If it's okay with you, we'll come to the city to see you twice a month."

"What the hell is this?" Michael says. "You're giving ultimatums now? Yesterday you wouldn't even talk to me about this, and today you're leaving me and taking Jasmine. Today *you* run the show? I don't think so. We had an agreement to talk over all decisions. You're violating that agreement!"

"Up to now," Ellen says, "you got 90 percent of what you wanted. You got to stay in the city 90 percent of the time and have the life you like. I only got 10 percent of what I wanted. I'm tired of losing all the time. Now it's my turn."

"And winning is everything, right? Is that what our relationship is, some kind of contest? Some battle that never ends? We're supposed to work things out, but you never say anything. This is crap, Ellen, and you know it. Jasmine is my daughter, too, and you cannot just take off with her. This is a war you don't want to start."

Ellen grows silent again and leaves the room.

Responses to Conflict

In a world in which physical resources are limited, survival goes to the fittest. The lion prevails if she is the most adept at attacking her prey. The rabbit prevails if he is adept at escaping an attack. Millennia ago, before the invention of central heating and super-markets, humans were more affected on a daily basis by this game of "survival of the fittest." We relied much more heavily on our physical resources for survival than we do now. Thus, as discussed in the preceding chapter, we developed a sophisticated series of physiological reactions to help us flee or fight our attackers and our prey, as necessary. Nowadays, because most of us who live in developed nations don't have to spend the bulk of our time and energy foraging or hunting, our fight-or-flight instinct exhibits itself in our competitive responses to conflict. Moreover, as our societies have grown more complex, these survival tactics have evolved into social strategies: "Fight" has turned into *aggression*, and "flight" has become *avoidance.*

In our social context, *aggression* is used to gain advantage over an opponent. When we act aggressively our intent is to harm our opponent and, thereby, to reduce that opponent's chances of win-ning. Some of the aggressive behaviors used in conflict include attacking, violent explosions (verbal or physical), shouting, insult-ing, and seeking revenge. There are also behaviors that we may not think of as aggressive, like "setting the other person straight," using sarcasm, or nagging. See our list of aggressive behaviors, below—some of them may surprise you. They are considered aggressive because they fit the definition of helping us harm, gain advantage over, or hinder our opponent.

Avoidance is the evasion of a conflict, as when we run away in a conflict situation so that we are not harmed. Complaining behind an oppnent's back, leaving the room, "killing them with kindness or politeness," becoming ill, and distracting oneself with other tasks or concerns are all examples of avoidance behaviors. The table below also lists some common examples of avoidance behaviors.

Aggression/Avoidance Behaviors

AGGRESSION (FIGHT)	AVOIDANCE (FLIGHT)
Attack	Escape
Explode violently	Dwell on how unfair they are
Shout	Complain behind their backs but say nothing to their face
Talk over the other person	
Interrupt	Withdraw physically
Insist you're right	Go silent
Try to prove your point	Get depressed
Nag	Get sick
Set the other person straight	Act super-polite
Issue ultimatums	Tell yourself you're not being fair if you say something
Get even	
Make caustic or biting comments	Busy yourself with something else, hoping the problem will go away
Hurl insults	Tell yourself it doesn't matter anyway
	Take it out on someone else

An aggressive response style has its advantages in the face of a less powerful opponent, but the advantages are often short-lived and overshadowed by the consequences. In the case of Ellen and Michael, Michael's aggression was verbal, ranging from a "debate to prevail" style of discussion to ridicule and name-calling. Yet Michael thinks of himself as a caring person and wants the best for Ellen and their relationship. He may be unaware that he intends to hurt, but the tactics themselves have that intention by design.

The major disadvantage to using an aggressive tactic is that violence (aggression) begets violence (aggression). Ellen turned Michael's "argue to win" strategy into a winning tactic for herself by declaring it useless and unfair to respond to him, and making her own decision.

Although conflict avoiders often appear to an onlooker to be more peaceable, avoiding conflict does not return either person to a state of peace. Ellen tried to avoid engaging in conflict with Michael for years, yet the conflict remained. Neither of them was getting their needs met, and both were unhappy. The only thing she succeeded in avoiding was engaging with Michael.

Finally she couldn't tolerate the situation anymore, so she mustered up her courage and struck an aggressive blow of her own. Michael's response was a more heightened, emotionally laden aggressive response, which she succeeded in avoiding once more by growing silent and leaving the room.

Assertiveness: A Third Way

What can you do when you and another person seem stuck in a conflict, trading places between acting with aggression and avoidance? Fortunately, there is a third way, and it's called *assertiveness*. Assertiveness is neither fight nor flight. It is a response to conflict with the intention to cooperate—to create a solution that meets both people's needs. It is not backing down. It is standing up for one's own needs. It is not destroying the opponent. It is seeking to understand the other person's needs. Assertiveness is the resolution of the fight-or-flight dilemma.

An assertive response to conflict requires that you take responsibility for your own needs and feelings. It may also require that you take responsibility for those of your actions that have contributed to the conflict. Assertiveness holds the greatest possibility for reaching a win-win solution and returning to peace. Let's take a look at a conflict where assertiveness was used.

Yasmine, a coaching client of Gayle's, brought up a conflict she was having at work with a coworker, Charlie, and their boss, Eric. As she described it, her coworker, who was new to the organization, was undermining her with their manager. Where Yasmine had once enjoyed an open and productive relationship with the boss, now, four months after Charlie's arrival, she found herself blocked from access to him. These days, she and Eric speak infrequently, even about business issues, yet Charlie can often be found meeting with him. And though she and Charlie have a good deal of work in common, she feels snubbed by him and stays out of his way.

The first thing Gayle asked Yasmine was if she had spoken to either Charlie or Eric about her concerns. Because her style of handling conflict is primarily avoidance, Yasmine had concentrated on watching the behavior of the two men, taking in certain office "information" provided by others, and generally feeling miserable about the situation. But she was aware of her style and how it had impacted her in the past, so when Gayle suggested she assertively confront the situation, Yasmine quickly agreed. The only question she had was how to do it most effectively.

Gayle suggested she speak with Charlie and Eric individually and let each one know what it was about their behavior that was of concern to her. Gayle also encouraged Yasmine to examine her own needs before speaking with them, as we did in the exercise at the end of Chapter 1. Upon reflection, Yasmine discovered that her needs for affiliation, belonging, and job security were all at the root of her conflict. She agreed to speak with Charlie that week, and during her next call with Gayle she would report how it went.

"It was amazing," Yasmine said the following week. "I asked him if we could have what might be a tough conversation about the way we were *not* working together. At first, Charlie didn't really want to talk about anything, but I remembered that assertiveness means taking responsibility for my share of what is happening, so I told him that I knew *I* was not working well with him. I told him I used to be the one who had strategy conversations with Eric and that I was feeling out of the loop. I said I wanted to find a way for us to at least develop a common ground for working together since so much of our work had the same focus. I think Charlie was stunned initially, but then he said, 'Yeah, I know what you mean. I really didn't know how you fit around here. I see you as my primary competition, but that doesn't mean we can't work together.' "

Charlie then told Yasmine that she had not acknowledged a big win he'd had with one of the company's largest accounts during his first month. Everyone in the office had congratulated him, except Yasmine. To him that meant she wasn't interested in a good working relationship; it was a sign of war. Yasmine acknowledged Charlie's work at that point in the conversation. She told him that he did do a good job and gave several honest reasons for her opinion. She then explained that the same day he received accolades for his work, Eric informed her that she would not be getting the raise he had requested for her. She apologized for not having acknowledged Charlie's good work and explained that she had been distracted by her own situation. Though she didn't admit it to Charlie, she told Gayle that she had been frightened by the combination of those events.

As they continued to talk during that week, Charlie admitted to Yasmine that Eric had told him that he was bothered by the lack of communication between the two. Eric felt that many of Charlie's questions could be better answered by Yasmine and was concerned that Charlie was only speaking to him.

During her conversation with Charlie, Yasmine used several of the assertive techniques listed below.

Techniques for Assertive Conflict Resolution

* Using opening statements/questions
* Active listening
* Identifying the other person's needs and feelings
* Expressing one's own needs and feelings
* "I" messages
* Creating the "we"
* Reducing defensiveness

Techniques for Assertive Conflict Resolution
(cont'd.)

---

* Reframing the situation
* Brainstorming
* Joining with the other person as a partner in solving the problem you face together
* Looking for win-win solutions
* Agreeing to disagree

In this case, being assertive required that Yasmine open the conversation with Charlie. She expressed her feelings of discomfort and her need for them to have a better working relationship. By voicing the idea that their work had a common focus, Yasmine created the "we" perspective to help work through the conflict. When Charlie described his feelings of distrust (which he didn't state explicitly, but rather implied) as originating when Yasmine failed to acknowledge his work, she actively listened and demonstrated that she was doing so by acknowledging him in that moment. She also helped to reduce his defensiveness by sharing some information about her own work situation that coworkers don't usually share (the fact that she didn't get an expected raise). In later chapters we will discuss in detail how to implement many of these techniques for assertive conflict resolution.

Toward the end of Yasmine's coaching session, she told Gayle that she was ready to speak with Eric. Being open with Charlie had had such a positive effect on how they worked together that she was ready to give it a try with her boss. She expressed a sense of relief at being able to end the tension between Charlie and her, and she was surprised by how frightened she had been to confront the situation.

As we will see in the next few chapters, assertiveness is a key element in the communication and problem-solving skills that foster peaceful resolution. But making the choice to respond effectively requires creating new habits to replace old behaviors.

Choosing Our Responses to Conflict

We all have unique styles of responding to conflict. Our styles are often different at home than they are at work. We respond differently to family, friends, children, coworkers, bosses, and strangers. Most of the time we respond to conflict without thinking about it, from habit. We form our habits in many ways: by imitating the response styles of our parents or other adults who helped raised us, from our childhood peer groups, as a reaction to situations we faced as children, by responding to adult pressures to behave in certain ways, and from illustrative media and TV programming. Much of the time these habits reflect some form of avoidance or aggression.

Remember Ellen and Michael's conflict about where to live? Ellen's habit of avoiding conflict came as a reaction to the violence in her family. Her mother raged uncontrollably when the children left their clothing lying around. Her rage usually resulted in a beating. As a small child, it was wise for Ellen to duck when her mother became angry. She continued ducking conflict as an adult, even though her physical safety was no longer at risk.

Michael, on the other hand, developed his aggressive conflict habits from imitating his father. His father would ridicule and bully family members whenever he got angry with them. Ridicule became the norm that Michael followed without even realizing he was doing it.

If we are aware of our habitual response styles, we stand a greater chance of freeing ourselves from habit and choosing to respond to conflict productively. However, during intense conflict we often feel as if we lack control over our responses. Our actions seem automatic and often feel unproductive.

Humans experience an eight-second delay after an incident occurs that can potentially evoke the strong emotions that send us into fight or flight. During those eight seconds our capacity to think improves and our physical reactions are suppressed. That's why folk wisdom—and advice from some behavioral experts—advocates counting to ten before responding to an incident that produces strong emotions. Doing so creates a window of opportunity to make a choice. It is only the first window, not the last, but it's an important window.

After those eight seconds, however, our thought processes are suppressed and all activity is centered in our body. We are off to the races in fight or flight. We discharge. We attack or escape. When that is over, our physical reactions are suppressed once again. We are tired. Our thinking grows clearer, but at that point we likely experience remorse for what we have just done.

Chapter 3 discusses in detail several strategies for taking advantage of this delay to change how we respond to conflict. The rest of this chapter explores the often deep-rooted sources of conflict within us.

The Physiology of Fight or Flight

In his book *Emotional Intelligence* Daniel Goleman describes a phenomenon he calls *emotional hijacking*. Emotional hijacking sets off the fight-or-flight response. Dealing with emotional hijacking is often the key to being able to successfully navigate the everyday conflicts we encounter.

A look at the physiology of the brain can give us a clue about how emotional hijacking occurs, what conditions trigger it, and what we can do to either prevent it from being triggered or return ourselves to a state of inner peace once it has been triggered.

According to Goleman, our brains are still wired the way they were three hundred thousand years ago. At that time the conditions under which creatures lived meant that they had to make quick judgments about which other creatures were a threat to survival and which were food. They had to act on those judgments with as short a reaction time as possible. The creatures that evolved were the creatures that developed the quickest and most accurate brain functions for reading and evaluating the environment and sending signals to the body to react. Our emotions are the names we put to those evaluate/respond reactions.

Emotions continue to be adaptive for us. They provide the impetus that motivates us to make important decisions. They are sources of information about the potential impact of an event on our lives. Emotions working in balance with reason give us clues that a need we have is being either fulfilled or thwarted. If our physical safety is threatened, we are likely to respond with fear. If our need for love or belonging is threatened, we are likely to feel sadness or grief. If our self-esteem or ability to act effectively in the world is being threatened, we are likely to experience anger. We can use these uncomfortable feelings as cues to evaluating situations and making decisions.

Unfortunately, many times before we even get a chance to think about what we are feeling, we are already reacting. We're wired for fight or flight before the intellect gets involved.

To understand the relationship between emotion and thought, it is useful to look at the brain's anatomy. The part of the brain that evolved first among ancient creatures was the brain stem, which rests on the top of the spinal cord. The brain stem is responsible for a variety of basic life functions, such as breathing, metabolism, and some very primitive survival reactions.

The next part of the brain to evolve was the olfactory lobe, located on top of the brain stem and responsible for the sense of smell. The sense of smell provided creatures with their initial method of evaluating stimuli and reacting to them—a relatively simple form of emotional information-processing. Are you an enemy? A meal? A sexual partner? The olfactory lobe sorts these stimuli and sends messages to the rest of the body: run, attack, chew, approach.

Ringing the top of the brain stem is the next set of neurons that evolved: the limbic system. These brain structures add sophistication to the olfactory lobe's emotional abilities. The limbic system is able to learn and remember. With the development of emotional memory, the olfactory lobe can work with the limbic system to make fine discriminations between smells, based on past experience. Together they can fine-tune the body's reactions based on these discriminations.

Thinking was further developed when the brain evolved the structures called the *neocortex*. The neocortex is a more complex web of neuron pathways. Forming the largest part of the human brain, piled on top of the previously developed structures, the neocortex has the ability to strategize, plan, imagine, create, and, in general, make subtle and flexible discriminations. The larger the neocortex, the more complex the system and the wider the repertoire of responses to a stimulus.

In the neocortex lies the ability to think abstractly. Language is rooted there. The neocortex helps us give words to our feelings and to sort them out based on a complex system of comparisons between past experiences and present circumstances. The neocortex allows us to choose our responses to our feelings from a complex array of possible responses—in other words, to think before we react.

What Triggers Fight or Flight?

The fight-or-flight response can be set off by several different stimuli. Let's take a look at some of them.

Danger

Of course, we *don't* always think before we react, and this, too, has an anatomical base.

Imagine a hunter in a jungle. He hears branches break, looks up, and sees a tiger in the trees. These messages are carried from his ears and eyes to the thalamus in his brain. The thalamus sends signals to a structure in the limbic system called the *amygdala*. The amygdala, which is our emotion headquarters, evaluates the stimuli (tiger—danger—fear) and sends emergency messages to all of the parts of the brain that control the varied body responses (flee/freeze/fight). It tells the brain to mobilize the body's troops immediately, if not sooner.

Most of the message (tiger) goes from the thalamus through the neocortex (rational thought) before it reaches the amygdala (feeling). This long path provides the person with a complex understanding of the subtleties of the situation, including the varied options for responding. *(The tiger is not looking at me. If I stay perfectly still, perhaps the tiger will go away.)* This is a quality pathway, but it takes some time for the messages to be carried through all those branches of brain cells.

However, in a world where reaction time could make a difference between dying and living to procreate, evolution provided a shorter route. At the same time that the thalamus sends most of the messages through the neocortex, a smaller number of messages are sent directly to the amygdala along a short path that circumvents the neocortex entirely. This emergency route allows the amygdala to mobilize the body's reactions immediately. The benefit is short reaction time, but since the route sidesteps the neocortex's subtle reasoning abilities, the disadvantage is that some emotional reactions take over without benefit of reason.

Danger: Short-Circuiting Reason

TRIGGER	PHYSIOLOGICAL RESPONSE
An immediately dangerous event can bring us to the heightened emotional state that sets off fight-or-flight signals.	When an event occurs, the thalamus records it and sends messages through two routes at the same time: 1. *the long path*—through the neocortex (where it acquires language and rational thought) to the amygdala (which interprets it and mobilizes the brain and body to react); and 2. *the short path*—directly to the amygdala (without going through the neocortex), generating a quick reaction before thinking sets in. The amygdala's interpretations and reactions make up our emotions. Most of the time, rational thought and emotions are in balance. However, if the amygdala interprets the event as dangerous, it quickly mobilizes the body for survival (fight or flight), shutting down rational thought.

When feelings are particularly strong, the amygdala sends out emergency signals to the body to pump up all functions that will help it react in the recommended way (approach, avoid, attack, etc.). It minimizes the bodily functions that are not directly in service of the recommended action. In other words, the amygdala, the seat of emotional thought, takes over. Essentially, the amygdala has hijacked the body in service of fight or flight.

A scene from *The Women of Brewster Place*, by Gloria Naylor, demonstrates an extreme example. A woman was raped and left bleeding in an alley by her male assailant. A male friend found her there and approached her to help. In a blind rage the woman got up, grabbed a two-by-four, and beat her friend unconscious, then sank in a heap against a wall, sobbing. The woman had been emotionally hijacked and struck out against violence with misdirected violence.

Most of the time our fight-or-flight response does not result in acts of extreme violence. We usually respond with forms of violence or escape that are verbal or social rather than physical. We get angry, and we may strike out verbally. We are fearful, and we may retreat from the situation.

Memories of Past Trauma

Events that call up memories of trauma can also set off fight or flight. As a result we fight ghosts instead of the real person or situation at hand. For example, Sheila was in a serious auto accident thirty years ago. She could not get into a car for a long time afterward without sweating and shaking. After a while Sheila was able to reeducate herself, but to this day every time she is a passenger in a car she experiences a great deal of anxiety.

Such broad-stroke comparisons served our early ancestors well. A tiger was always dangerous, whether it was the same one we saw when we were young or a different one, and whether it was in a tree or on a rock ledge. It was always appropriate to flee or hide or throw one's spear at the tiger if it was about to strike.

These quick reaction times to grossly similar stimuli were evolutionarily appropriate, but are less necessary now. In our complex and rapidly changing social structures, we have to be able to make the fine discriminations necessary for choosing the best response. We have to be able to overcome unconscious emotional hijacking so that we can mobilize our fine-tuned thinking process, and know the difference between the present situation and past danger.

Memories: When the Present Feels Like the Past

TRIGGER	PHYSIOLOGICAL RESPONSE
Events that call up memories of trauma can set off fight-or-flight reactions and cause us to fight ghosts instead of the actual person or situation at hand.	The amygdala stores emotional memories. These are primitive, broad-stroke associations lacking detail.

An emotional memory contains vague characteristics of the stimulus, of the amygdala's interpretations, and of the amygdala's reaction instructions to the brain and body.

- Emotional memories formed from *long-path* (conscious) reactions have language and rational thought attached to them. *Short-path* (unconscious) memories do not.

- Strongly charged memories are stamped deeply into our brains. The amygdala retrieves them easily.

- A present event can prompt the amygdala to retrieve the memory of a strongly charged past event that had vaguely similar characteristics.

- The amygdala reacts to the new event as if it were the same as the old event.

- If the old event held some real danger (trauma), the fight-or-flight reaction will be set off.

Early Childhood Traumatic Memories

Early emotional trauma is an especially potent source of the fight-or-flight response. Gary's mother was physically abusive when she got angry. She beat him frequently. When Gary was a small child this beating was potentially dangerous, yet it came from the woman upon whom he also depended for life-giving nurturing. He learned to find corners of the house to hide in when his mother got upset.

Now, however, at age fifty-five he is still finding corners to hide in when his lover gets angry at him. He has left relationship after relationship when issues became intense enough to provoke anger in the woman he was with. He does not trust angry women.

Childhood: Hidden Memories

Trigger	Physiological Response
Unconscious memories of early childhood trauma can leave us feeling emotionally hijacked without knowing what's happening or why.	The amygdala is almost fully developed at birth. The neocortex develops more slowly, taking a couple of years to begin to form language. Memories formed before the neocortex has fully developed are emotional memories that do not have language or reasoning attached to them. If the past events that formed these early memories signaled danger to the baby, the fight-or-flight response is set off in the adult when they are retrieved in the present, as if the adult were in danger now. Since these early memories are unconscious, a person can believe that the emotion experienced (fear, anger, etc.) is an outgrowth of the present circumstance and that the fight-or-flight reaction makes sense.

The strength and persistence of Gary's reactions to women's anger is not surprising, as the first imprint for fear took place early in his development. When Gary's fear is triggered as an adult, he has no set of words or thoughts to explain his reaction; he has only his chaotic feelings. Since the early memory was traumatic, its imprint on his brain is strong and his fear response is easily aroused. The stimulus that arouses it is an angry woman whom he loves, a stimulus that bears similarities to his early trauma, but only in broad strokes.

Anger is an emotion that inevitably rises out of conflict. Since conflict is inevitable in any relationship, long or short term, it is likely that Gary will be unable to find a woman who never gets angry. Much of Gary's reactions have more to do with ghosts from his past than with the present. In the past he was in physical danger, and the fear was justified and adaptive. In the present he is a six-foot-tall man whose physical welfare is not being jeopardized. Yet the fear that arises prevents him from being present to the situation at hand.

Since the emotional mind enlists the rational mind for its own purposes, we come up with explanations or rationalizations about how and why our feelings are appropriate in the present circumstance. We may feel certain that we know exactly what is going on, while we really have no idea that some past feeling has been triggered. Gary's escape reaction dominates his thought processes. The feeling is strong, so it feels real. He uses this reaction to justify his retreat. Instead of looking at the real sources of the present conflict, perhaps an argument over where to go on vacation, he is thinking about how this woman is dangerous, and how he must get away from her.

From time to time we all fight ghosts in our conflicts. A person or a situation can trigger the unconscious memories of past trauma, and we remain totally unaware that this has happened. A key to regaining our balance of emotion and thought is to simply notice that an imbalance is present. The clue is the strength of the emotion in the absence of immediate physical danger. If you can notice the imbalance, then you have already engaged the neocortex. Engaging the neocortex changes the physiology. It quiets the amygdala's takeover. It allows you to delay your reaction long enough to cool down the body's responses so that reason is no longer under the dictate of emotion alone. You can then obtain balance, and the neocortex's full capacity for making fine discriminations and strategizing accordingly can work alongside your feelings to help you choose an action.

Escalating Conflict Spirals

Joe, a teenage boy, is watching TV on the couch in the living room. His books and papers are spread all over the floor. His mother, Paula, walks in. "Would you clean up your stuff?"

"Sure," he says, and she walks away.

A few minutes later she comes back. Joe and all his stuff are still in the same places.

"Joe, didn't I tell you to clean up? Get up, now!" Her voice shows she is annoyed.

"Just a minute, Ma. This is the good part. Can't I do it later?"

"It's always the good part. This happens all the time. Stop being such a couch potato."

"You don't have to be mean. I said I would do it." His voice is raised.

"You're calling me mean? Don't talk to me that way!" She is yelling now.

"You yell at me, and I can't yell at you?" he shouts.

"I'm your mother!" she shouts louder.

"Big deal." He looks at her with a smirk.

"That's it. No more TV." She pulls the plug and carries the TV out of the room.

He leaves through the front door, slamming it behind him.

That was a scene from an escalating conflict spiral. The original conflict was minor, but by the end tempers were out of control and a lot more was at stake than some papers on the floor of the living room. How did it get out of hand?

The best way to counter an escalating spiral is to catch it as the level of emotional arousal is growing, before we are emotionally hijacked. If we can halt the progressive buildup of anger before rage ensues, we have a chance to cool ourselves down and rethink the situation.

Spirals: Tempers Rising

TRIGGER	PHYSIOLOGICAL RESPONSE
A series of upsetting events occurring close together can build to an emotional hijacking.	An anger-provoking thought or event becomes a mini-trigger for amygdala-driven surges of hormones called *catecholamines*, which escalate the body's arousal. The arousal subsides after a few minutes.
	If another angry thought comes before the arousal subsides, then the arousal escalates even more.
	Emotional flooding occurs when one surge builds on another, until the level of arousal is as strong as a danger response. Fight or flight is set off.

Once we have reached full-fledged rage, however, the most primitive limbic reactions set in. Unchecked rage can lead to serious forms of aggression or escape. If Joe and his mother had realized that each successive comment was fueling the other's anger, they could have halted the interaction before it got out of hand, taken a breath, and started over. However, as is often the case in an escalatory spiral, it happened very fast. They were left with further damage to their relationship that they will have to deal with once tempers have cooled.

Emotionally Charged Moods

Emotional hijacking can also be triggered by a minor conflict, if the conflict occurs during a series of unrelated upsetting events.

Ingrid left her job a few weeks ago in a huff after an argument with her colleagues. The argument was a typical one that annoyed her, but until then she had handled such episodes successfully. Ingrid is a hairdresser who rents space in a salon. There is frequent bickering among the other hairdressers about sharing the salon's upkeep and record keeping. The latest argument occurred after Ingrid returned from her brother's funeral.

One week before the argument, she had left work in a hurry because she had a date. She wrote out a check for the rent but neglected to sign her name. All her colleagues were upset about it. To them this reflected the haphazard way she typically dealt with paperwork, a habit that sometimes caused problems with scheduling clients. David, one of her colleagues, was charged by the other hairdressers to discuss the matter with Ingrid. In the interim, Ingrid's brother died, and Ingrid took a week off from work.

When Ingrid returned, her colleagues expressed their regrets at her loss, and each of them spent some time hugging her and talking with her before starting the day. However, half an hour later David approached Ingrid and told her that everyone had asked him to speak to her about her record keeping.

Ingrid looked at him in disbelief. "What?" was all that she could say.

"You didn't sign your name on the rent check when you left, and we all had to contribute to cover for you."

"What? So, okay. Sorry. Where's the check? I'll sign it."

"Well, it's more than that."

"What?"

"This is just another way you messed up your paperwork that inconvenienced all of us."

"So that's how it is." Ingrid was close to tears. Normally this argument would have been like any other annoying day at work for her, but now, in her heightened state of emotional arousal, she couldn't deal with it. "I won't inconvenience you anymore!" She scooped up all her supplies and packed them quickly into two shopping bags.

"Ingrid. Ingrid…." David tried to stop her, but Ingrid was out the door in a few short minutes. She never returned. Emotional flooding led to impulsive flight.

If David had been aware that Ingrid's emotional state left her more susceptible to emotional hijacking, he could have waited until another time to approach her about the paperwork issue. If Ingrid had been aware that she was more susceptible to emotional hijacking, she might have avoided conflict situations altogether until she felt better. However, life does not always cooperate with our needs, and sometimes conflict enters our lives even while we are trying to avoid it. Ingrid felt she had to return to work, and the conflict was waiting for her there. Still, her awareness of her susceptibility would itself have engaged her neocortex and helped to cool down her reactions. She could have paused and caught herself before making any rash decisions she might regret later on.

Charged Moods: The Straw that Breaks the Camel's Back

Trigger	Physiological Response
The presence of a major upsetting event that is affecting your mood can cause a minor event to be blown out of proportion and set off emotional hijacking.	The release of catecholamines after an upsetting event has two effects: 1. a surge of emotional arousal that lasts for a few minutes; and 2. a ripple through the adrenocortical branch of the nervous system, which for days puts the body in a general state of readiness for further arousal. If a normally minor irritating event occurs during this second arousal state, the person's feelings can be easily hijacked.

Ruminating

Engaging the neocortex through thought and reflection usually helps to cool down emotional flooding. However, not all thought processes have that same beneficial effect. Rumination, a circular thought process, may only prime the emotional pump, flooding it and bringing on emotional hijacking.

For a moment let's return to Gary, who tends to run away from female anger. If Gary dwells on his fear without any awareness that the source of his fear is rooted in the past, his thoughts might play out like this:

How could she talk to me like that? She's dangerous. A mouth like that. Why do I always seem to get hooked up with these violent women? I thought she was sweet. Next she'll go for the jugular. I can't trust her. This is real bad. And look at how she's insisting we spend our vacation in the mountains. She doesn't care about what I want at all! How can I trust her? She's only out for herself. God, I've got to get away from this woman. Why would I want to vacation with her anyway? I don't know what will come out next. What nerve—to talk to me like that!

With each thought he feels a greater dose of fear, until he has talked himself into an emotional hijacking. Then he's in flight.

Ruminating: You Are What You Think

TRIGGER	PHYSIOLOGICAL RESPONSE
After even a relatively minor event, you can talk yourself into getting emotionally hijacked if you dwell on the event without seeing a solution.	Since the primary message path for emotional response is the long path through the neocortex to the amygdala, a thought can trigger an emotion.
	Thus, a disagreement can trigger a mildly emotional thought that is balanced by rational thought.
	Rumination on the disagreement primes the feelings, intensifies the reactions, and eventually floods the thinking function—bringing on emotional hijacking.

If we are aware of the signs of emotional imbalance as they occur, we can pull ourselves out of the vicious cycle of rumination. First, we can add empathy. We can begin to see the person we are reacting to as someone who is struggling to survive, like we are, even if the survival struggle leads them to behave in difficult ways. Empathy helps to cool us down, quiets the fear or the rage, and brings us more information that can lead us out of the circle of rumination. Empathy can lead us to a more balanced state of mind, from which we can analyze the situation and begin to search for solutions. For more about empathy, see Chapter 4, including the exercise.

Reframing the situation—seeing it in a new way—also changes the circular nature of the thinking process. With rumination, our thinking loops back to anger or fear. With reframing, our thinking moves to analytical, hopeful thoughts that have the possibility of leading to a solution. The focus is on the present conflict as a problem to be solved rather than on the other person as a threat. Reframing is an example of an assertive technique for conflict resolution. Recall the discussion in Chapter 1 of positions versus needs in a conflict. One way to reframe a conflict, as discussed in that chapter, is to look deeper than each person's stated positions for his or her underlying needs.

A possible reframing process for Gary might go as follows:

> She got angry. I don't like the way she talked to me. We've got to deal with that. We also have to deal with this issue about where to go on vacation. She wants to go to the mountains, and I'd rather go to museums. But her reaction to the issue was so strong that I wonder if it's really about the two weeks we spend on vacation, or if it's about something bigger than that for her. We need to work something out that satisfies both of us.

Pausing to Think

Whenever we are triggered into fight or flight, the first step is to notice that we have been set off. Do this by taking advantage of the eight-second delay described above to pay attention to what is happening in your body. You may find yourself breathing quicker, sweating, becoming flushed, feeling a knot in your stomach, tensing your muscles, having thoughts of attack or escape, or experiencing a general feeling of unease that seems out of proportion to the situation. These are cues. If we can notice the imbalance between the seriousness of the situation and our physical, mental, and emotional reactions to it, that act alone will engage our thinking process and begin to restore the balance between our thoughts and our emotions.

If you are aware that you habitually either avoid conflict or act aggressively in the face of conflict, then it's possible to catch yourself in the act—to say to yourself, "I'm running away again," or, "I'm ready to attack again." Recognizing your habit—and the intense feelings that accompany it—allows you to pause and reflect. This readies you to take the next step: cooling down, discussed in Chapter 3.

Knowing your pet peeves, those situations that commonly set off fight or flight for you, also provides opportunities for you to pause before you do something you might regret later. For example, Gayle can get very upset when she believes someone is taking advantage of her. So when she feels this is happening, she makes a point of stopping, stepping back, and verifying whether her feelings reflect the reality of the present conflict. She withholds judgment until she can cool herself down. Self-knowledge gives us pause to think. We need such a pause so that, instead of being emotionally hijacked, we can begin to restore balance and choose the most effective response to the conflict.

The roots of conflict run deep, but becoming aware of the why and how behind your actions signals the beginning of a new response. Recognizing that your reactions to stressful encounters are built in by nature to protect your well-being is part of the self-knowledge so important to conflict resolution, but it is only part of what is necessary for effective solutions. In addition to recognizing your habitual physical responses, you must use your thinking brain to take control of your emotions and find a balance between thought and feeling. As a part of this thinking process, you realize that there are a number of other factors that can trigger the fear response: factors created by your own mind as you relive past traumas or compound small annoyances into larger problems.

Once you recognize what is happening when you respond to conflict, you can begin the process of changing your reactions in search of more thoughtful, productive resolutions. Doing so starts with a moment, a pause.

ℬ Exercise: Identifying Triggers

The best way to identify the things that set you off—your triggers—is to pay attention to your day-to-day life. To do so, keep your journal or a notebook and a pen handy.

1. On the first several pages of your journal, create three columns. Title the first column "Triggers," the second column "Feelings," and the third column "Responses."

2. For the next week, carry your journal with you. In the first column, jot down the words, phrases, and behaviors that trigger you. It's important that you use simple words and phrases as identifiers. Do not identify a particular person as your trigger, but rather the behaviors, words, or gestures that set you off. For example, your list might contain the following: (a) having my dinner interrupted by a sales call, (b) shouting, (c) eye rolling. Notice that there is no indication of who exhibited the behavior.

3. Sometimes whether or not a behavior is a trigger will depend on who exhibits the behavior. For example, a child strongly voicing an opinion may be a trigger, whereas it wouldn't have the same impact if it came from an adult. Make note of these differences when you experience them.

4. At the end of the week, review your list of triggers. In the second column, write down next to each trigger how you feel when you encounter that behavior. Your list might include emotions ranging from frustration to rage to sadness to fear.

5. Place an asterisk (*) next to any trigger that initiates rage, fury, anger, powerlessness, or hopelessness. In the third column answer the following questions: How did you deal with these triggers when they arose? Specifically, what did you say or do in response? See if you can find your response listed in the table of Aggression/Avoidance Behaviors at the beginning of this chapter.

6. Take some time to read and reflect on each of your responses to the triggers marked by an asterisk. Are these responses typical for you in reaction to that trigger? If not, write down other responses you have had to this trigger.

7. As you read, ask yourself if these behaviors helped to create peace in your relationship, or did they cause more aggression, avoidance, and conflict? Put a check mark next to each response that helped to create peace, and an X next to each that hindered it.

The more we know about our conflict triggers and our habitual responses to them, the closer we are to changing behaviors that hinder resolution. In the next chapter we will describe several techniques for managing our responses to triggers. We'll look at ways we can begin to short-circuit aggression and avoidance by regaining our center, which will allow us to begin moving toward assertiveness.

CHAPTER 3

𝓟𝓪

Cooling Down and Centering

The artists who sell their paintings on the streets of New Orleans' French Quarter share a space along a fence. There are no official reserved spots, but over the years the artists have come to informal agreements about rights to particular spots. A newcomer, Lisa, set up her paintings for two weeks in a vacant spot. She was told that Paula might appear any day to reclaim her spot.

Paula showed up with her paintings late one afternoon and tried to reclaim her spot, but the other artists advised Lisa not to move. Paula, they explained, was too late that day to claim her spot. The rules the artists had agreed to months before stipulated that a person had to show up by 11:00 A.M. in order to retain her or his "spot" rights for that day. Paula could set up in the spot next to Lisa.

Paula stomped around, banging her canvases along the sidewalk, snapping the bungee cords loudly as she fastened the canvases to the iron fence, and pinching her flushed face into a pout in Lisa's direction. Lisa could feel her limbs tense, and a knot distressed her already hungry stomach. Feigning calm, she sat with her back to Paula, but inside she was ducking an imagined threat.

After Paula finished hanging her paintings she strode over to Annette, the artist who told Lisa not to move. Paula shouted at Annette about her spot, and Annette shouted back about the rules. The two went head to head. A crowd gathered to watch the fight—two red-faced women chopping the air with their hands, screaming. Lisa sat silently in her imagined bubble. All three women were in fight-or-flight mode.

John stepped in and whispered to the dueling women, who looked up, noticed the crowd for the first time, and moved away from each other. The crowd dispersed. It took the intervention of a third party to help these two notice that they needed to change their actions.

Paula moved back to her artwork. She and Annette spent the next few hours chain-smoking cigarettes and talking incessantly about the incident to nearby fellow artists until the story lost its power over them and they settled back into the business of selling their art.

How to Use This Chapter

This chapter will help you develop the skills of cooling down and centering. By breaking down the process into small practical steps, you'll start to become aware of the choices you may be making unconsciously. Carefully read through this chapter and think about an unresolved conflict from your past, or a conflict in which you are currently engaged. How might things have worked out differently if you had used some of the techniques outlined in this chapter?

At varying points in the chapter there will be exercises for you to do. Take your time and complete them before moving too far forward into the book. These activities will provide you with techniques that you can use when you are in a conflict. However, they need to be practiced first to be effective. Practice them once or twice from the book, then try them out when you feel annoyed or frustrated by someone's behavior or by a circumstance that is not a strong trigger for you. Note: *do not* practice these techniques while driving.

To illustrate these techniques, we'll return to the conflict between Paula, Lisa, and Annette, our New Orleans artists.

Step 1: Notice the Cues and Your Habitual Responses

As discussed in the final section of Chapter 2, cues that you are on the brink of a fight-or-flight response (or are already fully immersed in one) include *physical* sensations such as sweating, tense muscles, a knot in your stomach, and a quickened heart rate and breathing; *mental* processes such as thoughts of lashing out at the other person (aggression) or of fleeing the scene (avoidance); and *emotional* intensity that seems all out of proportion to the actual danger at hand. Familiarize yourself with the pattern of cues and responses you tend to follow when faced with conflict. As you learn more about your conflict cues and responses, jot them down in your journal. For example, Gary, the man described in Chapter 2 who tends to flee from women's anger, might observe that his fear of women's anger causes him to sit silently or to leave the room when a woman expresses anger at him, and to break up with a woman soon after they've had their first serious fight.

For Paula and Annette, noticing the cues required the help of a third party. Their *fight* response, which took the form of verbal aggression, was visible. By contrast, Lisa's *flight* response, avoidance, would have been visible only to a third party deeply acquainted with the situation. Many people misinterpret the flight response. Since the individual often remains quiet, avoids eye contact, and speaks calmly, others may make the assumption that nothing is wrong. Therefore, Lisa's response did not bring about an intervention from another person. In her case, knowing her own cues could have helped her catch herself in flight.

Step 2: Pause

The next step is to stop the fight-or-flight activity by pausing to think, another skill touched on in Chapter 2. Once we are aware of our physiological, mental, and emotional response patterns—our cues—we can begin to think about what is happening and how we are reacting. After realizing that Lisa was not going to move, Paula might have asked herself a few of the following simple questions: *Is this a trigger? Do I always respond to this trigger with aggression? What is usually the result? Which of my needs underlie the conflict? Why is that space so important to me, right now?* Taking the time to answer questions such as these would have helped Paula gain control over her response. Ask yourself these same questions when confronted with a conflict, and write down your answers in your journal.

Paula's overtly aggressive response was directed at Annette. When she separated from Annette, her overt fight behavior stopped, but she was still angry. Through her body language and facial expressions, she continued directing covert hostile attacks toward Lisa, the artist who had set up where Paula usually did. Lisa got the message and felt that hostility. Having witnessed Paula's screaming match with Annette, she was afraid that Paula would scream at her. Since Lisa had been subject to much screaming accompanied by beatings while she was growing up, her fear froze her in flight mode. She continued to sit alone, facing the other direction, despite her growing desire to talk to Paula and work something out. Had she been able to stop her flight response, she could have softened her body language and tried to make eye contact. Likewise, a softening of body language on Paula's part could have helped Lisa approach her. Unfortunately, they were both still captive to their fight-or-flight instincts.

Step 3: Cool Down

To unhook yourself from fight or flight, you need to actually change your physiology (your body's physical mobilization) in order to stop the emotional hijacking. During the fight-or-flight response your body's physiology is working to make sure you are ready for action. Blood is pumping to your extremities at a fast rate. Breathing is rapid and shallow. Muscles are tensed, ready for combat or quick retreat. All this activity produces heat. You feel flushed. You sweat. Here are some ways to change your physiology either when you first notice the cues that signal impending fight or flight or once you find yourself in the midst of a full-blown fight-or-flight reaction:

Cool the Heat

One way to calm down is to literally cool your body. Both Annette and Paula found themselves unconsciously reaching for some water to drink after they separated. If you are aware that you need to cool down, or if you are helping someone else cool down, common methods for doing so include splashing your face with cool water, fanning, or taking a cool shower.

Return Breath and Pulse to Normal

Deep abdominal breathing can serve to slow the pulse rate and restore shallow, rapid breathing to normal. Try the following exercise:

℘ *Exercise: Abdominal Breathing*

1. In order to observe what a shallow, rapid breath feels like, try breathing rapidly with shallow inhalations and exhalations. Usually in a rapid, shallow breath the upper breastbone rises and falls, but not always. Sometimes the breath is so shallow that movement of the breastbone can barely be noticed at all.

2. Inhale slowly through your nose, visualizing the breath going to your abdomen. Be conscious of how your diaphragm or midriff is filling and rising with the inhalation. Placing a hand on your diaphragm can help you retain awareness of your breath.

3. Exhale through your mouth, being conscious that your diaphragm is contracting as you breathe out.

4. Take a few deep, slow abdominal breaths in this way, then observe as your breath returns to normal.

5. At first, practice abdominal breathing while you are alone. Then practice breathing this way while you are engaged in activity or among people. Practice doing it subtly, in a way

that does not disrupt the activity or call attention to your breathing.

6. Next time you are in a heated conflict, if you feel your breath becoming rapid and/or shallow, say to yourself, "Breathe deep," and allow yourself to take a few deep abdominal breaths. You can ask for a moment to pause, and use that time to take three deep breaths. If you don't get a moment, and you have been practicing deep breathing, then you can automatically shift your body into deep abdominal breathing, even while you are in a heated debate. It will clear your mind and help make you more effective.

Discharge Bodily Tension

Because during conflict your body is tensed to enable you to either attack or retreat, if the tension remains in your body your muscles continue to send attack or retreat messages to your brain. These messages can skew your thinking process, creating a series of thoughts that you may not act on but that nevertheless affect your approach to the situation (for example, "I want to get him!" Or, "I'd like to see him fry!" Or, "This is a dangerous person. I'm out of here!").

The tension in your body can be discharged through physical activity and/or relaxation methods. Often people intuitively develop their own methods for releasing tension. I have heard people say that when they get angry they take a walk, punch pillows, stretch, do yoga, sing or hum, dance, play tennis, play basketball, ride a bike, put on soothing music and relax, put on wild music and boogie, take a bubble bath or a shower, swim, and countless other activities.

These methods are only possible if you can get away from the situation that is causing the conflict. However, sometimes you are prevented from getting away. The situation forces you to deal with the conflict on the spot. The following is an exercise that can help you release the tension in your body even in the heat of a conflict.

If you practice this exercise at home while you are not in conflict, you can summon the relaxation effect during a conflict and experience a release of muscular tension.

♥⌅ Exercise: *Muscle Relaxation*

The first time you try this exercise, get in a comfortable position, either sitting or lying down, away from distractions.

1. Tense up all the muscles in your body, and keep them tense for a count of three.

2. Release the tension. Breathe out quickly through your mouth.

3. Tense up all your muscles, this time noticing your neck, shoulders, arms, hands, legs, and feet. Take a mental survey of each of these areas, one at a time. Notice how they feel when they are tensed up.

4. Release the tension. Breathe out quickly through your mouth. Now breathe regularly. Take a mental survey of your neck, shoulders, arms, hands, legs, and feet. Notice how they feel with the tension released.

5. Tense up all your muscles. This time notice the same muscles you noticed before, but add to the mental survey your face, throat, chest, abdomen, spine, back, and buttocks. Really notice each part as it is tensed up, as if you are studying how it feels in that state.

6. Release the tension. Breathe out quickly through your mouth. Notice how all your muscles feel with tension released, this time adding to the mental survey your face, throat, chest, abdomen, spine, back, and buttocks. Notice carefully how each feels relaxed.

7. Practice steps 1–6 a few times.

8. At some point during the normal course of the day *when you are alone*, make a mental survey of all your muscles. If

you feel tension in any of them, give them a mental message to relax. Notice the muscle(s) relaxing. Try this a few times.

9. At some point during the normal course of the day *when you are engaged in activity or conversation,* try taking a quick mental survey of your muscles. Wherever you find a point of tension, give the muscle a mental message to relax. Try to do this and at the same time *still remain engaged* in the conversation or activity that is going on. Practice this a few times until you feel you have mastered it.

10. Next time you are in a heated conflict take a quick survey of your muscles, telling tense muscles to relax. This will aid your clarity of thought and your ability to choose the most productive course of action in solving the conflict.

Take Space and Time, If Necessary

Sometimes the best cool-down method is taking time or getting away from the person with whom you're in conflict. Distance from the triggering event allows the body's functions to return to normal on their own, provided that your own rumination doesn't feed the flames. It's like taking a vacation from the conflict so you can come back refreshed. However, be aware of the temptation to take a permanent vacation once you feel comfortable with the space and time. That is, be aware of the temptation to avoid the person or the subject of the conflict altogether. Taking space and time can easily end up as the flight response in disguise. When you are in flight, nothing gets resolved. Hurt feelings fester. Problems remain that can reemerge. You can lose valuable relationships. Take a vacation if you need to, but come back.

Step 4: Return to Your Center

We have talked about the physiological imbalance between emotional and rational thought that can be created during conflict, and we have talked about the need to restore balance so that we can think and act clearly and choose the most productive responses. Many of the recommendations in the preceding section, "Cool Down," will help restore your physiological functioning to normal. Remaining balanced throughout a difficult situation is the next challenge.

Many disciplines discuss the state of being "centered," each with its own interpretation about what the term means. Some refer to a physiological center or to a psychological, emotional, or spiritual center. In general, though, all these disciplines seem to refer to being centered as the state of thinking clearly, feeling fully, and reacting in one's own best interests and the best interests of others—that is, the state from which a person can resolve conflict assertively. Being centered means being one's best self. If we can remain centered throughout a conflict situation, then we stand a chance of creating an outcome that returns both parties to a state of peace.

Many years ago, Sheila was in the middle of a difficult conflict with an intimate friend. They agreed to have a phone conversation on a certain evening. The day before they were scheduled to talk, Sheila was nervous all day because it had been her experience that every time she tried to deal with difficult subjects with this person she would get very flustered—thrown way off center—and would end up either yelling or withdrawing altogether from the conversation. When she stayed in the conversation, she usually failed to express herself well. Her words came out all wrong. This time she wanted to express herself clearly and calmly and make the right decisions for this relationship.

That same day, while browsing in a bookstore, Sheila came across *Warriors of the Heart*, by Danaan Parry. In it she found the following exercise, used by practitioners of aikido (a martial art) for finding their center of gravity, which Parry also calls the *power center*. Parry recommends the exercise for remaining centered during conflict resolution as well as during martial arts combat. Sheila practiced the exercise that night and the entire next day. That evening, during the conversation with her friend, she was able to remain clear and focused. They worked out a resolution. The centering exercise became a tremendous help to Sheila, not only in conflict situations, but any time she was under stress and needed to think and act clearly and effectively.

℘ *Exercise: Finding Your Center of Gravity*

1. Stand with your feet shoulder-width apart and close your eyes.

2. Put your fingers three finger widths below the navel.

3. Now rock back and forth gently and imagine the back-and-forth line your fingers are making.

4. Return to a still position.

5. Now rock from side to side gently and imagine the side-to-side line your fingers are making.

6. Imagine the point at which the two lines cross, the intersection. That is your center of gravity.

7. Return to a still position, centering yourself on that intersection.

8. Open your eyes, remaining aware of it.

9. Now walk around the room. Look at everything in the room, but at the same time practice remaining aware of your center of gravity. Maintain a dual focus.

10. When you are in conversation with people or in the middle of any activity, practice drawing your attention to your center of gravity and remaining aware of it while you are still engaged in conversation or activity.

If you practice maintaining the dual focus, then in conflict situations you will automatically remind yourself to draw your attention to your center of gravity and retain awareness of it during the process of trying to engage the other person in productive conversation.

Step 5: Observe Yourself

Observing the self—that is, becoming aware of your intentions and your behavior—is another way to help you regain balance and return to your center. Do this by shifting your attention away from the conflict and toward your own internal mechanisms. Become aware of your tone of voice, posture, emotions, and intentions. Then, with the information, feelings, and understanding brought about by viewing the situation with emotional and mental distance and awareness (what some disciplines call *detachment*), a more balanced choice can be made.

Let's revisit the image of the tiger, this time in the story of a monk who is being chased by a tiger and finds no way of escape except up in the weak branches of a tree. With the tiger circling below and the branch where he is perched about to break, the monk looks around him and sees the most beautiful blossom. The blossom, he decides, is where he will focus his attention. Though aware that he will soon be facing the tiger, he controls where his mind takes him. Contemplating the beauty of the flower is his choice.

Most of us would be filled with fear knowing the tiger waits below, just as we are often filled with fear, anger, sadness, and disappointment when in the middle of a conflict. One way to center ourselves while maintaining an awareness of our situation is to look for what is good or beautiful in the situation. Doing so is a good way to remind ourselves that we have choices.

Gayle and her eight-year-old daughter had been struggling over homework. It was an exceptionally beautiful day. Summer in Atlanta was approaching an end, and the air was cooler and less humid than it had been in months. Her daughter, Sky, who knew that the rule of the house was "homework first," rushed through her math problems so she could get outside.

As Gayle checked Sky's work, she found that eight of the twelve problems were wrong. All of the errors were minor, but the answers were incorrect. So, in keeping with the rule, she informed Sky that she would have to continue working until the problems were corrected. Large and plentiful tears began to emerge; after a summer at theater camp, Sky's ability to add dramatic flair was in full display.

Sky's tears pushed Gayle's buttons. "The rule is the rule, it's not arbitrary," she said. "Your job is to learn, just like I have a job. Let's get back to work." Sky responded with, "Blah, blah, blah."

At that point Gayle saw red. Although she was in excellent health, her blood pressure surged upward. "Don't you dare...," she began.

But as she started to answer, Gayle became aware of two things: that her voice was rising, and that she loved Sky. It was the loudness of her voice that got her attention and keyed her in to the fact that she was acting unconsciously, or without awareness. She was acting without first *choosing how* to act, and the conflict was escalating.

Sky plopped into her chair at the kitchen table and showed only her profile. Gayle calmed her voice and said, "Sky, look at me. I know it's nice outside and you want to ride your bike before it gets too late, so here's the deal. Let's work through half of the problems you've done wrong, take an outside break of forty-five minutes, and then come back in and finish your homework." Though Sky wasn't immediately convinced that this was the best plan (she lobbied for two corrected problems and then a break), within a few minutes they were back on track, and within fifteen minutes both were outside enjoying the sunshine.

An important point is that Gayle did not lose her awareness of what was at the core of the conflict. Sky's completing her homework continued to be the need that Gayle had to have met. However, she was also able to consider meeting Sky's need once she regained her center.

While she used several conflict-resolution skills in her interaction with her daughter, the key element was that Gayle was able to regain her center by observing herself. For a brief moment she stepped outside of the conflict. First she observed that the volume of her voice had increased, then she allowed an awareness of her love for her daughter to guide her response. It was, after all, her love for Sky that contributed to Gayle's need for Sky to learn.

Step 6: Come from Your Heart

Both cooling down and centering help people in conflict to temporarily detach themselves from the strong feelings that can set off destructive fight-or-flight behaviors. However, in order to retain the balance between emotion and thought you have to be very connected to your feelings. Feelings provide important information about yourself and others. They help you evaluate what is occurring. They tell you if your needs are being met. They allow you to empathize with the other person so you can perceive their needs. If you detach yourself from your feelings altogether and operate solely from the rational mind, a different kind of imbalance will occur.

Danaan Parry offers an extension of the centering exercise described above to help people connect their physical center of gravity to their heart center. This exercise enables you to keep your heart open to your feelings and to the feelings of others while remaining centered throughout the negotiation of a conflict.

৭৯ *Exercise: Connecting Your Heart Center to Your Center of Gravity*

1. Stand with your feet about a foot apart. Fix your attention on your physical center of gravity. Place the fingers of your right hand against your center.

2. Bring your left hand up to cover your heart. Place it over either your physical heart or your heart center, in the middle of your chest, whichever feels more right to you. (Parry considers the heart center to be the center of love.)

3. Imagine a channel connecting your heart center to your physical center of gravity.

4. Breathe deeply, and as you breathe, imagine that the channel is deepening and that energy is flowing from your center of gravity (your power center) to your heart center (your love center).

5. Imagine that power and love are connected, so that your actions are strong and centered, and at the same time are informed by a knowledge of feelings and a sense of love for yourself and others.

6. Practice this exercise while alone and while you are interacting with others until you have mastered the dual focus between these internal centers and the activities in which you are engaged.

7. The next time you are in conflict, bring your attention to your power center, your heart center, and the channel that connects them both; at the same time, retain the focus on the conflict negotiation in progress.

It takes some time to learn the methods of breathing deeply, releasing tension from your body, finding your power center and heart center, and connecting them. However, once they are mastered, it is fairly effortless to pull it all off in a moment. All you have to do is remember to send a message to your body to breathe, relax, center, and retain the dual focus. Your body, mind, and heart will respond without missing a beat, and you can engage the other person in conversation in your best, most powerful, balanced, and caring way.

Step 7: Engage Your Thought Process

In a cool, centered state it becomes possible to engage your thought processes so you can choose the best course of action in the present conflict. Whereas pausing (step 2) asks you to stop and observe your behavior, this step asks you to specifically examine your thoughts and change them, if necessary. Do this by noticing your reactions and relating them to possible patterns of thinking. Have you been engaging in circular thinking or rumination that is fanning the flames of emotion and keeping you stuck in fight or flight? Are you particularly emotionally susceptible at this time? Could that be influencing your reaction? Has there been a progressive buildup of anger that may be causing you to overreact now? What is your habitual response to conflict? Are you being aggressive or avoiding the conflict because that is your habit? Is there another strategy that might work better now? Engage your rational thought processes to take another look at the situation, to reframe it in a way that might help you change your circular thinking, and to separate the past from the present.

Let's return to Paula and Lisa's conflict about where they each were entitled to set up their art. They found a resolution much later that day. It took time and space away from each other for both of them to calm down enough to think about the situation and be ready to speak to each other. Over the course of the day, Lisa became increasingly concerned that she needed to talk with Paula. She felt that although she had been following the instructions of the more senior occupants of the "fence," her presence had caused the upset, and it was incumbent on her to try to work it out. She had become increasingly aware that she was avoiding talking with Paula, and she knew that avoidance of conflict was a habit from her childhood. She knew she had to break out of the avoidance mode, but as long as Paula continued to be hostile, Lisa's fear kept her from approaching Paula. However, a fortunate occurrence eventually helped Lisa approach Paula. Paula made a big sale, which changed her mood and her countenance. Feeling the shift in mood, Lisa was able to summon the courage to approach Paula.

Her first approach was to make eye contact and smile. The smile was met with another smile. Then Lisa walked over to Paula and said, "Hey, lets talk about this situation with the spots." It was a conversation opener.

"This spot has been mine for two years now," Paula replied. "I haven't been coming out for the past two weeks because I was taking a break."

"It's confusing to me, because if you are going to come out sporadically I will never know whether that spot is free," Lisa said. "The spot you are in right now belongs to someone else, so I don't know where to set up."

"Well, it was settled a long time ago that we have reserved spots, and I want to keep mine where it is since my customers look for me here."

"If I know when you're coming out, I won't set up that day."

"Usually I come out every weekend."

"If there's a particular weekend you plan not to come out, let me know and I can set up there."

"Okay. And if we're all out on the same day, then we can move our stuff over a little and squeeze you in so we can all set up along this fence."

It was a win-win solution that seemed to have the potential to work. What made it possible was a combination of time and space to cool down, a fortunate situation creating a shift in mood, and some internal reflection on Lisa's part about her habitual avoidance and the need to overcome it. A cool, centered discussion between the two occurred that took both people's needs into account.

Recognizing the cycles of conflict, understanding the way your brain functions, and knowing what triggers your emotions are all-important to peaceful resolutions, but your ability to quell your emotions, center yourself, and reengage your reason are absolutely vital to your ability to achieve positive outcomes. If you can develop the skill of pausing in the first moments after your emotional brain floods your body with adrenaline, you are well on the road to a reasonable, measured response. But doing this can be quite challenging, especially if you already have habits of aggression or avoidance. The exercises provided in this chapter can help build the skills needed to respond in the moments after a conflict erupts. Without the ability to calm down and think things through, you will remain at the mercy of your emotions. Once you have acquired this skill, however, you are ready to move on to new levels of conflict resolution, such as letting go of blame, discussed in the next chapter.

Chapter 4

℘ᴙ

Letting Go of Blame

Working on a project with Inter-Change Consultants, Sheila consulted with a large technology firm. Her responsibility was to provide expertise in the development of a human resources training manual. She worked closely with Judy and Dave, members of the company's human resources department. Judy was responsible for writing the first draft of the manual; Dave's role was to edit it.

The editorial meeting between Dave and Judy was long and arduous, filled with disagreements and hostile feelings. It was the first time they had worked closely together, and they weren't used to each other's style. Judy disagreed with many of Dave's suggestions and felt that Dave was trying to impose his will on her. Dave felt that Judy was being uncooperative and undermining his efforts. It was a clash of personalities, but each tried to blame the other when they discussed the problem with their supervisor. Work on the project was stalled, and deadlines were missed.

The supervisor, making a subjective decision, took sides with Dave and laid the fault for stalling the project at Judy's feet. Judy, seeing that the conflict was getting out of control, appealed to the supervisor. She said, "Please, let's just try to find a ground of agreement and get back to work." However, it was too late because plans had already been put in place to replace Judy in her role.

Blame

Dave and Judy's experience, as well as the actions of the supervisor, point out an important principle underlying peaceful conflict resolution: It is never productive in a conflict situation to try to place blame—to put energy into finding out whose fault it is. The goal in resolving conflict is to find a solution that meets both parties' needs.

There are situations in which it is important to determine who is guilty, who is innocent, who is right, or who is wrong. In other words, sometimes we need to place blame. For example, if a crime is committed, it is important to find the guilty party—the thief, murderer, etc. Our legal systems are constructed to aid this pursuit. Detectives gather evidence. Witnesses are part of the evidence. Criminal lawyers take their client's side and line up evidence and witnesses to prove their client's case—to prove guilt or innocence. Lawyers are called *advocates* because they advocate for one side of the blame question. Judges hear the evidence and, in certain circumstances, decide guilt or innocence. In other circumstances they remain neutral, interpreting the law for the jury, whose role is to pass judgment.

The court system is very ingrained in the collective psyche of our culture. This fact is reinforced by the popularity of detective and courtroom dramas and of "whodunit" mysteries. Many of us automatically go into that mode of thinking when approaching a conflict. However, a law-enforcement approach to interactions, whether at work, at home, or in friendships, does not result in peaceful, productive relationships.

When a dispute arises, no matter how severe, blame fails to solve the problem. It makes the conflict worse by generating more hard feelings. If two people are unable to solve a conflict, most likely each of them is contributing in some way to the difficulty they are having. In some way they are both culpable. It is better to drop the search for blame altogether and focus attention on cooling hot tempers in order to discover underlying needs and reach a win-win solution.

Empathy

When we are angry at a person, our tendency is to project negative motivations onto her or him. In the heat of our anger, we often believe the worst about the person. In cases of extreme anger and emotional hijacking, we will dehumanize him or her in our minds.

During the unpleasant editorial process between Judy and Dave, the anger progressively built between them until they were both quite miserable. Later, in conversations with friends about the situation, Judy referred to Dave as "the Nazi." Dave referred to Judy as "that undermining b———." Neither could see the other's point of view. They could no longer deal with each other face to face. Instead, they approached their supervisor about interceding on their behalf. This just made matters worse. In conflict, the more one uses potentially biased intermediaries instead of dealing directly with the other, the stronger the tendency becomes to dehumanize the other person and see them as the enemy. (More on this topic is presented in Chapter 16.) When one is fighting an enemy, aggressive and retaliatory tactics feel justified. Defeating the enemy can become the goal. It is war.

Judy and Dave's dispute arose out of disagreements over the changes in the document. Their different communication styles created a situation in which misunderstandings blocked the communication that might have helped them resolve their disagreements. To develop peace in their work relationship, they needed to be able to break through the misunderstandings and see each other's deeper underlying needs. The conflict needed to be reframed, so that instead of focusing their energies on placing blame, they could work together as partners to find mutually satisfactory (win-win) solutions.

The words we use to describe the other person in a conflict reflect our willingness either to create peace or to engage in a win-lose struggle. References to "adversaries," "enemies," "Nazis," "b_____s," and the like all evoke images of two people working against one another. Recognizing the other person as your partner in the effort to resolve a conflict requires empathy. Empathy can be described as the ability to recognize the universal similarities between yourself and another; to acknowledge and appreciate each other's needs and points of view; to see the other as a person worthy of respect; to see oneself in the other. When two people are in deep conflict, sometimes empathy disappears and they are unable to appreciate each other. If a third party intervenes to help resolve the conflict, one of the first tasks would be to help each party gain a deeper understanding of the other—that is, to help create resonance. Resonance is the feeling of being understood by and connected to another person. When both parties recognize that differences exist between them that create conflict, and when each is willing to work toward understanding the other's perspective, they have achieved resonance and started a conflict-solving partnership.

The Drowning Person

Many years ago, Sheila received a swimmers' lifesaving certificate from the American Red Cross. The course taught her that when swimming toward a drowning person in an attempted rescue, the rescuer must be vigilant and prepared for a common occurrence: that the drowning person will lunge at the rescuer's head and grab it in order to save himself or herself. This action could potentially drown both the rescuer and the one being rescued. It is not a rational action. It is destructive, but it is an automatic survival response.

Similarly, during intense conflict when emotions are running hot, sometimes people do and say things to each other that are destructive to both parties and to the possibility of creating peace. In the absence of rational thought, destructive tactics may take over, because something has set off a person's internal "danger" signals and it feels as if her or his survival is at stake.

It is tempting when we are in conflict with someone who is acting difficult and destructive to either retreat from the situation altogether or to retaliate with similar tactics. However, if we can remember the drowning-person analogy and understand that in a psychological sense the other person may feel like he or she is "drowning," then it is possible to maintain empathy for that person.

In Sheila's Red Cross course, the trainees were taught to approach the drowning person with a particular swimming stroke that allowed them to quickly retreat if the drowning person lunged at them. Similarly, in conflict, even if we are able to retain empathy for a destructive person, it is unwise to stay in the path of destruction. If the other person is doing you harm either physically or psychologically, then move out of the way.

The lifesaving trainees were taught several different methods for bringing the drowning person to shore—methods of approaching, holding, and calming the person so both people would be safe and so the rescuer could swim to shore while holding the drowning person. These methods were difficult to learn and required a great deal of practice before the trainees became proficient at them. Part III of this book addresses a number of communication skills that can potentially calm a hostile person with whom we are in conflict. However, these methods also require quite a bit of practice before we are skilled enough to deal with a person acting in a severely destructive manner.

The trainees were also taught that sometimes they would be unable to use the recommended methods to bring the drowning person to shore by themselves. In that case, there were other methods they could use without endangering themselves to ensure that the person wouldn't drown. They could throw the drowning person a ring buoy or other object to grab. The rescuer could get another person to help out. In conflict, if we are able to retain empathy for the other person even in the face of their destructive actions, then we may discover ways in which we can get help in calming and centering the person so that the destructive actions are diminished and we can begin to resolve the conflict. Sometimes an objective, capable third party can intervene to help calm the person and turn their actions around, so that they are receptive to negotiating peace. More on the topic of third-party intervention in conflicts is discussed in Chapters 13 and 16.

Self-Awareness

Conflict can potentially be navigated peacefully with the help of an awareness of your own needs, habitual conflict patterns, triggers, and cues. In order to be able to calm yourself down and remain centered while retaining empathy for the other person, you need to have a degree of self-reflection and awareness. This book recommends a certain stance toward one's own actions: to be an observer of the self; to examine your present actions in light of your habitual patterns; and to conduct that self-examination by bringing your personal history and the forces that shaped you into your conscious, rational mind. Although self-observation can often be accomplished on your own, sometimes practices designed to increase awareness, such as psychotherapy and meditation, can help.

Self-awareness involves looking at oneself with a degree of honesty. Sometimes in the course of self-discovery, we may react by blaming ourselves for our own destructive actions. It is important that we extend the same measure of empathy toward ourselves that we extend to others—that is, to examine our own actions without self-blame. Each of us is subject to forces in our lives, in our histories, in our physiology, and in our psyches that shape what we do and how we perceive what is happening. We need to understand and forgive ourselves as well as others before we can get on with the effort of creating peace in our relationships.

In our culture of competition, we seem naturally inclined to find someone or something to blame when a conflict is not effectively resolved. Our legal system focuses on passing judgment, determining guilt, and assigning blame, but, as mentioned earlier, this model for approaching conflict is less effective in our personal lives. By assigning blame, we create a win-lose scenario that gets in the way of a mutually satisfying solution. Blame blocks progress. Instead, we must seek ways to produce win-win outcomes. Two powerful tools to peaceful resolutions are available to all of us: empathy and self-awareness. If we can develop a deeper understanding about what makes us tick, we will find that understanding others' positions is much easier, too. As self-awareness and empathy grow, it becomes much clearer that, in a very tangible way, we are all in a similar circumstance—and it has little to do with who is at fault.

℘ Exercise: Empathy

Have paper and pen handy.

1. Bring to mind once again the conflict you wrote about in the exercise at the end of Chapter 1. Review what you wrote down about the other person's position as you understand it.

2. Close your eyes, take a few deep, calming breaths, and summon a sense of empathy for the other person. If you think it would be helpful, first do one or more of the exercises described in Chapter 3: the abdominal breathing exercise, the muscle relaxation exercise, finding your center of gravity, or connecting your heart center to your center of gravity. You might also imagine that you are the other person, put yourself in their place for a moment, and try to view the conflict through their eyes.

3. Recall what the other person communicated to you both verbally and nonverbally during the conflict. Now ask yourself, "Based on the other person's communications, what is my best guess about *why* the other person wanted what he/she wanted?" Without editing yourself, write down whatever comes to mind. *Note:* It's important to realize that you're only making an empathetic guess about the other person's underlying needs. You may get it right, or you may get it wrong. The important element here is the attempt to understand the needs and feelings of the other person. The more you try to understand their feelings and needs, the greater success you will have in creating a conflict-solving partnership. When confronted with an actual conflict, you will have an opportunity to hear, understand, and accept

the other person's reality as *they* express it to you, and later chapters will provide methods for improving your ability to do so. For now, making an informed guess is enough.

4. Distill what you wrote in step 3 into the *underlying needs* (psychological or tangible) you think the other person may have had. Express them in one or two words each. If you wish, review the table on pages 18–19 to help you come up with words that fit those needs. Again, remind yourself that you're only making an informed, empathetic guess.

5. Review the list of your needs (from the Chapter 1 exercise) and the list of the other person's needs. Brainstorm for a few minutes about how the two of you might have resolved the conflict so that *both* of you felt like you'd "won." For some ideas, review the win-win solutions presented toward the end of Chapter 1 for the conflict between Julie and Rose. The key is to remember that win-win solutions meet as many of both people's underlying needs as possible. Try to come up with at least two win-win solutions. Write them down. Over the next few days, more solutions might pop into your mind. Jot them down as they occur to you.

Part II

❦❦

Being Present

CHAPTER 5

Is the Conflict Really About This Incident?

In the previous chapter, Judy and Dave's conflict broke out during the editorial meeting and escalated from there. Each attempt to resolve the conflict seemed to make it progressively worse until neither one could speak to the other. It had grown into an out-of-control, escalatory spiral. Soon the situation seemed so complex that neither could pinpoint exactly what the conflict was about, because it had developed many layers. It was so complicated that it left both of them wondering what they were fighting about.

Often in complex conflict situations, we lose sight of what the conflict is really about. In any conflict it is important to ask oneself, "Are we fighting about what we think we are fighting about? Is this conflict really about what happened in this particular incident, here and now, between you and me?" In other words, "Are we in the present moment?" If two people in conflict with each other are not operating in the present, then it is difficult to discover what their underlying needs are and to generate solutions that feel acceptable to both parties.

In the next few chapters we will look at how, when, and why a conflict sometimes grows bigger than the particular event that seems to have triggered it. We will examine what could be called the "conflicts behind the conflict": patterns involving needs, people, and events from the past that color the way individuals respond to conflict in the present. We will also suggest ways to become aware of the history that influences a conflict so you can bring the conflict back to the present moment, making it possible to create win-win solutions.

When Conflict Escalates

Destructive responses to conflict can create a *conflict escalation spiral*. One unresolved conflict leads to another, each time raising the level of tension and emotion until a long history of unresolved conflict is built up. In a particular conflict, it may be necessary to examine the steps that led up to the triggering incident in order to identify what you are fighting about. You may be fighting over prior conflicts instead of the present issue.

Bruce has an office at home. His fifteen-year-old son, Jordan, asked Bruce to take him shopping to buy a pair of jeans just as Bruce was about to be immersed in a lengthy long-distance conference call. Besides feeling a serious time crunch, Bruce was also annoyed at the request because Jordan knew that his mother said she would get him the jeans. Bruce felt, however, that if he told Jordan he wasn't going to take him shopping, Jordan would try to engage him in an unpleasant battle. Bruce did not want to deal with that now, so he responded to Jordan's request by saying he'd think about it if Jordan cleaned his room as he'd promised.

About an hour later Bruce's twenty-year-old daughter, Tanya, needed to be dropped off at her part-time job. That was a task Bruce had promised to do. He interrupted his call, promising he'd call back within fifteen minutes. Just as Bruce and Tanya were leaving, Jordan came downstairs and said he wanted to go with them.

"Did you clean your room?" Bruce asked.

"Yeah. I did it."

"So, let's go, quick," and they all got in the car.

Bruce thought Jordan was just along for the ride, so he was surprised when after Tanya was dropped off Jordan asked, "Where are we going to park?"

"Park? Why would we park?"

"To get the jeans."

"I didn't say anything about getting you the jeans."

"But I cleaned up my room like you said. You said you would get them for me if I cleaned up my room."

"I said I'd think about it if you cleaned your room. You didn't say anything about the jeans when you got in the car. You just assumed I would stop. I have to get back. I'm in the middle of a conference call."

"But you said if I cleaned my room you'd take me shopping for the jeans. It's not fair. You're always doing this."

"You had no right to assume I would go shopping with you, just because I was going in the car. You always do this."

The argument continued like that, heating up until they were both very angry at each other. Then fate intervened. The car stalled. Bruce had to have it towed. It was hours before he got back to the conference call, and, needless to say, Jordan didn't get the jeans. The anger generated from the incident lingered through the rest of the week, creating tension between father and son and fueling numerous other skirmishes.

Let's look in more detail at the conflict between Bruce and Jordan.

Arguing over Positions Instead of Needs

The conflict-escalation spiral between Bruce and Jordan began with both of them arguing over their positions. Jordan's position was that he wanted his father to take him shopping for jeans. Bruce's position was that he didn't want to take Jordan. Neither of them spoke about their own underlying needs, nor did they inquire about the other's needs.

Bruce's need was for time to complete his work so that he could continue earning money for his family. That's a survival need. An additional need was to be able to engage in the phone conference about a satisfying professional project; thus, work satisfaction and self-actualization were also at stake. Bruce also felt that his son was trying to manipulate him into taking him to buy jeans when both of them knew that Jordan's mother had promised to take him. Bruce's need in this case was for respect and honesty from his son. He did not communicate his intentions clearly to Jordan because he did not want to take on the argument he thought would ensue. His need there was for peace of mind.

Jordan's need was for sharp clothes to wear to a party. There was a girl coming to the party whom he wanted to impress. So his deeper needs were for a positive self-image, social acceptance, and affection. Additionally, Jordan thought his father would take him shopping if he cleaned his room, which he did. He needed clear communication from his father about his father's intentions. He needed respect and honesty from his father as well.

One Side Losing

As the conflict progressed, Jordan lost. Bruce won. Bruce refused to take Jordan shopping for jeans. This created resentment on Jordan's part. Jordan accused his father of being unfair and brought up situations from the past in which his father had failed to come through on promises. This escalated the conflict further.

New Skirmishes Arising Out of Thwarted Needs

The fight then became about the past, each accusing the other and using harsh and insulting language. It was a whole new fight, not about the jeans, but about how each of them related to the other and kept (or didn't keep) promises. In addition, it became about how each of them was talking to the other right then, the harsh language creating a situation in which neither wanted to back down.

Although the shopping issue came to an end when the car broke down, each returned home angry and stayed angry. Their anger fueled fights between them for a few days, until Bruce's wife (Jordan's mother) intervened and asked them to sit down together and air their feelings. Because the family had a tradition of "family meetings," they were able to use this forum to talk about what was going on between them and end the series of skirmishes. In this case, a third party, loved and respected by Bruce and Jordan, paved the way for them to find resonance, and the family tradition helped them establish a conflict-solving partnership.

Jordan's mother did take him to buy jeans in time for the party, as she had promised. A truce was called.

Conflict Escalation and Thwarted Needs

Recognizing Underlying Needs

Let's take a closer look at needs and how to identify them. Psychologist Abraham Maslow studied and categorized human needs and motivations. He organized these as a hierarchy, because he believed that certain needs take priority over others. For example, if a physiological/survival need is not being met, then it takes center stage until it is satisfied, and so on up the hierarchy. As each category of needs is met, a person is, in a sense, freed up to focus on the next-higher category in the hierarchy. Self-actualization needs are at the top. Once all other human needs are met, a person can focus on self-actualization. However, self-actualization does not become important to a person until the other, more basic needs are met. See the drawing and table below for a summary of Maslow's categories of human needs.

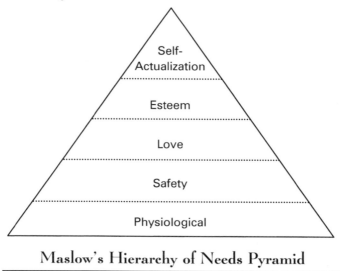

Maslow's Hierarchy of Needs Pyramid

Maslow's Hierarchy of Human Needs

CATEGORY OF NEEDS	DEFINITION
Self-actualization	To do our best, be our best, give our best effort in the achievement of a task or the fulfillment of a role or responsibility. Raising the bar on our accomplishments. This need is not activated until our esteem, love, safety, and physiological needs are met.
Esteem	Self-esteem and the respect or high regard of others. Once we have met our need for love and connection to others, we can turn our attention to meeting our needs for self-respect and the esteem of others.
Love, affection, and belonging	Connection to others, giving and receiving love, acceptance, caring, camaraderie, collegiality, etc. These can be addressed only after we have met our needs for safety.
Safety	Freedom from physical or psychological pain; a sense of order and stability. After satisfying our physiological needs we are able to address needs of safety.
Physiological/ survival	Basic needs like air, water, food, shelter, etc. These are the needs that must be satisfied before a person can consider other needs.

Other theorists subsequently disputed aspects of Maslow's theory, offering other categorizations and both anecdotal and empirical evidence to show that sometimes the needs on the higher rungs of the hierarchy take priority over the more basic needs. Some researchers assert that women have a different hierarchy of needs than men, and that therefore the two genders think and argue differently from one another. However, an important principle to be gained from Maslow's theory is that at different times, different needs have more importance than others. In each conflict a person has a variety of needs, though some needs feel more pressing than others.

Needs fall into categories, and if you probe enough you can discover the category of a person's needs. The categories are nearly universal among people. In resolving conflicts we must try to determine the variety of needs that exist for each person in the conflict and probe for underlying needs that might be hidden. For example, Jordan needed his father to follow through on what he perceived as his father's commitment to take him shopping. Underlying the need to go shopping was the need to be respected, which is the need for self-esteem. That's a need that Bruce shared. He could recognize his son's need for respect. In their discussion a week later, the acknowledgment of that need created resonance between them. They understood each other.

Priority of Needs Changes Over Time

In an escalating conflict the priority of needs changes over time. As the conflict proceeds, the more basic needs—that is, the needs lower in the hierarchy—often become more important. Sometimes needs arise because of *how* we are fighting. We saw that happen to Bruce, who went from needing time for his phone conference (money for survival and the self-actualization that he got from his work) to needing respect (esteem) once Jordan's communication became loud and angry. When needs arise because of the escalation of the conflict, they may take priority over the original needs in a conflict.

Jordan's initial need was to get jeans so that he could look his best (esteem). However, as the conflict progressed, his belief that his father was not following through on his promise became more important (love), and he became very angry. His father's response to him fueled his anger more, because he felt he was not being taken seriously in his request (esteem). In the end, his need for love and affiliation with his father took precedence, and he responded to his mother's encouragement to talk things out.

To attempt to resolve conflict when there is a series of escalating incidents, take into consideration that needs change over the course of conflict. Try to discover the underlying need that has become the most important for you and for the other person at that particular time. Thwarted needs that gave rise to the initial conflict still have to be discovered and addressed in any solution. However, be aware that sometimes the original need is no longer the priority.

The List of Atrocities

In long-term relationships, anger about unresolved conflicts can build up as partners carry around an ever-lengthening list of grievances about each other. We saw this happening with Bruce and Jordan when they brought up incidents from past conflicts. It often happens that by the time a married couple moves to divorce, they have accumulated so much past history of grievances that they have difficulty identifying when and where the rift began. Instead, there is a "list of atrocities." Changes occur in a relationship as the list of atrocities accumulates. Partners, spouses, or associates may be less willing to engage in certain activities together. These changes are called *structural changes*, and they reflect both parties' loss of faith, trust, and belief in the possibility of a peaceful resolution.

Bruce and Jordan's practice of "family meetings" was a factor that prevented a loss of faith from occurring in their relationship. They were able to keep communication open in the long run. However, in Judy and Dave's situation, there was no company practice that helped them keep communication open, so their lack of trust in each other grew. As the lack of trust grew they avoided dealing with each other. The more they kept their distance, the more the lack of trust increased, resulting in a vicious cycle, until each became the enemy in the other's mind. Once they started to feel the other was the enemy, aggressive blows felt justified. They each discredited the other to coworkers and supervisors. Dave went on a campaign to get Judy fired. Judy retaliated by filing a grievance against Dave. A successful intervention by a third party could have helped them find a ground of trust from the beginning, but by the time the grievance was filed, the structural changes had occurred. They had reached a point of no return. They would never trust each other again.

In marriages and other love relationships, sometimes the structural changes take the form of loss of affection and love. The bond that initially brought the couple together dissolves. All that's left is anger and the list of atrocities.

Dealing with Escalating Conflict

Next time you're involved in an escalating conflict, remember that the skirmish is not necessarily about that particular incident. It may be about the history of escalation that has occurred between you and the other party—that is, about all the conflicts along the way. If you are aware that your conflict has escalated, the following steps can help you return to the present moment and gain the motivation to bring the relationship to peace:

1. **Make sure you are in a quiet environment where you and the other person will have a sense of privacy.**

2. **Bring your feelings into the present moment.**

   Take a deep breath and ask yourself, "What am I feeling? Why am I feeling this?" These questions will help to ground you in the present. If your answer to "Why am I feeling this?" is because of something that happened between you and your conflict partner in the past, acknowledge it, at least to yourself. (Experience will tell you when it's appropriate to share.)

3. **Try to discover the most important needs for each of you at the moment.**

   Ask yourself, "What do I need right now?" If your answer is not easily identifiable as one of the underlying needs we identified in Chapter 2, ask yourself, "Why do I need that?" This will help you get closer to the underlying need and away from the position you may have taken.

   Before you share your needs with your conflict partner, ask him or her what they need from you right now. If you think they are expressing a position rather than a need, explain that you want to get a better understanding of what is happening. Then, ask them why they need whatever they have expressed. If you think you have heard an underlying need, state it. (For example, "I think I understand. You need me to respect you.")

As you begin to gain an understanding of their needs, also begin to express your own.

4. **Help both yourself and the other person develop an understanding and appreciation of each other by identifying underlying needs you both either share or can recognize. This will help to build empathy for one another.**

A statement as simple as "I can understand why you need _____" goes a long way toward building empathy. Asking the other person if they can understand your particular need is a little trickier. They may be unable to, and you should be prepared for that response.

Point out when your needs are the same or similar. (For example, "We both need to know that the other person cares about us.")

5. **In dealing with the history of the conflict spiral, see if any needs from the past have yet to be met. Try to discover needs that may have arisen through the course of the escalating conflict.**

Continue to check in with the other person, even though you may both be feeling better. Often, the good feeling that comes from establishing empathy and partnership in peacefully resolving a conflict can lead you to conclude that you have surfaced all the needs. Ask yourself and your partner, "How did this start? When did you first start to feel _____ (angry, frustrated, confused, curious, etc.)?"

If the conflict has been spiraling for more than a few days, it will take time to unravel all of the needs involved. Make sure you have adequate time for this conversation. In fact, you might suggest that the two of you continue talking about your needs over time. Agree to several more conversations.

6. **Above all, try to stop the escalating conflict spiral from progressing so far that a sense of hopelessness ensues and structural changes occur that prevent the conflict from being resolved at all.**

You may be the only one in the conflict who is aware of the escalation, or who has even a basic understanding of peaceful resolution. In this case, you will need to concentrate first on returning to your own center (using the exercises in Chapter 3) and on finding empathy for the other person (see Chapter 4, including the exercise). Then, using the steps outlined above, you can begin the process of ending the escalation.

It is often difficult to be the only person working toward peace in a conflict. If these skills are new to you, you may feel very uncomfortable and perhaps even vulnerable. Hang in there. Remind yourself that you are committed to working through your conflict positively and peacefully. Then, remember when, not so long ago, you also lacked an understanding of conflict—in other words, maintain empathy for your conflict partner. While there are some relationships in which structural changes are so profound that a resolution that would keep the parties together is impossible, most relationships can be improved and/or repaired.

ℱℛ ℱℛ

Losing track of an argument is a common experience. Without a satisfying resolution, more conflict arises, creating an escalating spiral of pain and disappointment. But the news is not all bad. A spiraling disagreement—if it can be stopped—may uncover hidden desires. A problem that begins with something very simple often reveals other, more important unmet needs. As the history of unresolved tension becomes clear, an opportunity arises to express past slights and recognize how needs naturally change over time. A failure to address both parties' underlying and changing needs can lead to unyielding problems for any relationship, reducing it to a "list of atrocities" that results in structural changes in a relationship. These changes lead to a loss of faith, trust, and belief that a peaceful resolution is possible. The goal of resolving conflicts must be to avoid that outcome by first dealing with the present needs of each person. Once the present problem becomes clear, you can begin to clear up past incidents that led to the current conflict.

⟡

CHAPTER 6

Is the Conflict Only Between Us?

Constituencies

Sometimes when you and I are in conflict, it isn't only between you and me. Sometimes we stand for others. Others have some interest in the outcome. When we directly represent other people, they are our *constituencies*. If we are negotiating a conflict on our constituency's behalf, their expressed desires and needs must be taken into account, not just our own.

For example, a union representative negotiating a contract with management is answerable to the union members. Likewise, the management negotiator is not representing his/her own position about the company's concerns. He is representing the position of the management team, CEO, board of directors, and stockholders. In this case, a conflict about pay raises and working conditions is not between the two negotiators. They are standing for others.

Standing for others has an effect on the conflict, whether the conflict is about everyday relationships or about formal contract negotiations. It tends to escalate the conflict in the following ways:

- **Resistance to resolution can increase** because the negotiators feel bound to represent the position(s) of their constituency. Therefore, the representatives become less flexible than they might be if they only had to answer to themselves. They become more fixed on positions, unless they are clear about the underlying needs of their constituency.

- **Disagreement among constituency members tends to make the process more unstable.** If the negotiation is complex and lasts a long time, the negotiators might have to go back to their constituency several times with new proposals. With each new proposal, an opportunity for disagreement arises among members of the constituency. Representatives might find themselves shifting positions in an attempt to represent the prevailing point of view as they address the newly surfaced underlying need.

- **Factions can emerge within the constituency,** such as between those who are more oriented to resolution (doves) and those who are more oriented to holding out for their position (hawks). Hawks and doves in a constituency can pull the constituency in either direction.

- **Representatives may feel a need to save face in front of their constituencies.** Representatives might realize that certain concessions are necessary in order to come to an agreement. However, they might feel that if they concede too much, their constituencies will lose trust in both the process and the representative. They may need certain concessions from the other side that would help them save face so they can retain the members' trust.

Invisible Constituencies

An *invisible constituency* can exist in a conflict that seems to be a personal conflict between two individuals. One or both people can be standing for others and be unaware that they are doing so. The overall tendency when visible or invisible constituencies are present is for conflict to escalate. For that reason—to short-circuit or altogether avoid a conflict escalation spiral—it is helpful to be aware of who else will be affected by the outcome of a conflict, and of what effect this constituency has on the intensity of the conflict.

In the Garfinkle household, parents Trisha and Doug set a curfew of midnight for their teenage daughter, Sonya, on weekend evenings. Sonya found herself repeatedly having to go home earlier than her friends. Sonya decided to ask her parents to make her curfew later.

Sonya's parents felt that Sonya's friends stayed out too late. Sonya was the oldest of four children. They were concerned that if they changed Sonya's curfew it would set a precedent, and that in the future they would find themselves pressured to allow their younger children to stay out later also. They were concerned not only for Sonya's safety, but also for the safety of their younger children. Though their younger children were not involved in the current conflict over curfews, Doug and Trisha were standing for their interests. The younger children were their invisible constituency.

Sonya also had an invisible constituency. Her friends had an interest in the outcome of the conflict between Sonya and her parents. If Trisha and Doug upheld the midnight curfew, the friends' parents might be influenced to make the curfew time earlier for their children as well. Sonya's friends were her invisible constituency.

Sonya initially raised the curfew question very quietly. Trisha and Doug did not act as if they were open to discussion. They answered without anger in an understanding but inflexible tone. They said the curfew would stay as it was. Sonya asked if they could please reconsider.

Doug was more inclined than Trisha to make the curfew later. He didn't mention this to Sonya, but instead asked Sonya to leave them alone to talk in private. Sonya did not realize that this was a sign that her parents' solid front was waffling. While she was waiting in the living room while her parents talked in the kitchen, Sonya complained to her younger sister, Paula, that their parents were being mean about the curfew. Trisha came into the living room fully prepared to make the curfew a half hour later, but Paula blurted out, "So are you going to give in?" This pushed the "constituency button" for Trisha. Instead of saying, "Yes, we're going to make the curfew later," she said, "It's not safe for young girls to be out after midnight, Paula. Sonya, your curfew is midnight."

The next weekend Sonya was staying over at her friend Jana's house. They were both going to a party. Trisha called and inadvertently mentioned to Jana's mother that Sonya usually had a curfew of midnight. Jana's mother told the two girls they had to be back by midnight. Jana was very upset that she had to come back earlier than usual and let everyone at the party know that it was Sonya's mother who made them leave so early.

The next day when Sonya came home she slammed the door behind her. She shouted very loudly, "Ma, why did you do that to me? Why are you interfering with Jana? Isn't it bad enough that I have to come home earlier than everyone? Why do you butt into other people's lives?"

Trisha, enraged that her daughter was speaking to her like that, yelled back, "You are my daughter, and you will come home when I tell you to!" Sonya's sister, Paula, was listening. For Paula's benefit, Trisha demonstrated the consequences for breaking curfew by adding, "And if you are not back when I tell you to come home, I will not let you go out at all!"

The conflict had escalated. The invisible constituencies, without ever being named, had had an effect on the conflict escalation. The conflict was not just between Sonya and her parents. All the sisters and brothers and friends and neighbors had a stake in the outcome and therefore influenced the course of the conflict.

Dealing with Invisible Constituencies

An important element in effectively dealing with invisible constituencies is to make them visible. What makes this difficult is that it requires the party with the constituency to be aware of the constituent's influence and to be willing to share that information with his or her conflict partner.

In the case of Trisha and Sonya, Trisha was aware that her other children's needs were also a part of the conflict. However, in making her decision, she didn't make Sonya aware of that responsibility to ensure the safety of Sonya's siblings, nor of her fear that she would be unable to fulfill that responsibility if she lengthened the curfew. Sonya also kept her constituency hidden, lobbying for the later curfew so that her friends' curfews would not be jeopardized. In this case, neither Trisha nor Sonya strived to be conflict-solving partners.

Remember that empathy is required for the establishment of a conflict-solving partnership. If Trisha had completed the empathy exercise in Chapter 4, she might have been able to imagine what it felt like for Sonya to always be the first of her teenage friends to leave a party or gathering. She might still have made the same decision, but she would have been able to express her understanding of Sonya's need for acceptance within her peer group. Additionally, in the spirit of partnership, Trisha could have shared her concern about Sonya's younger siblings, identifying them as her invisible constituencies. It would have been a good idea for Sonya to have engaged in the empathy exercise as well. Together, they might have come to a solution that met both of their needs.

When you are in a conflict and have constituencies, ask yourself if it is really necessary to keep them hidden. Surfacing your needs and the needs of your constituents makes resolution more likely. A willingness to consider the needs of your conflict partner's constituents establishes resonance and also moves the conflict toward resolution.

Identity Groups

We are all members of many *identity groups*. Identity groups include gender, family of origin, present family, nationality, ethnicity, race, geographic region, generation or age group, profession, religion, socioeconomic class, sexual orientation, and more. At times, when we are in conflict with another person, one or more of our identity groups become like invisible constituencies for us. We are not just standing for ourselves. We are also standing for the other members of our group, whether or not we intend to do so.

An engaged couple was in the process of looking for an apartment they could share in New York City. Sara said she wanted an apartment with a large, eat-in kitchen, a commodity that is hard to find in New York since space is at a premium. Lonnie put a high priority on a sizeable living room. It seemed impossible to get an apartment they could afford that offered both features.

The apartment-hunting process became emotionally charged for them. They looked at an apartment with a spacious kitchen that had a lot of counter space and plenty of cabinets for storage. Next to it was a separate dining area that led to a large living room. He felt sure the layout would meet her needs for a large kitchen, but she rejected it.

"The table can't go in the kitchen," Sara said.

"But it's big. There's plenty of room for cooking," Lonnie said.

"That's not the point. We can't sit in it."

"We'll sit in the dining area and the living room. Why is it such a big deal?"

"It just is. Why do you need a formal living room? What about that apartment we looked at yesterday?"

"The one with the kitchen in the living room? Not a chance. I hate that setup."

Neither of them could say why their preference was a big deal. They didn't really know why. It just seemed the way to do it. It felt important. It was about creating a home. Both of them had been sharing apartments with friends. The wedding date was drawing closer and still no apartment seemed right for them to share.

Her mother made a large dinner for both of their families—parents, grandparents, and the two living great-grandparents. At the dinner, the apartment hunt became a topic of conversation. The couple admitted they hadn't found one yet, but they didn't really want to discuss their arguments openly. Sara was grateful that her great-grandmother let her off the hook by drawing everyone's attention to her own tangential reminiscence.

"When your grandpa and I got married," said the great-grandmother, "who had money for an apartment? We lived in a furnished room together. But at least we had that. When I came here from Europe, I lived with my sister, her husband, and their four children in a cold-water flat on the Lower East Side. You walked into the apartment, and you walked straight into the kitchen. Everything was in the kitchen. The stove was in the kitchen, and it heated the whole house. The kitchen sink doubled as a tub. There were two tiny bedrooms off to the sides with doors right off the kitchen. Everything took place in the kitchen. We all sat around the table. The kids played on the floor under the table. At night, two chairs were pushed together with a feather quilt on it. That was my bed."

The two fiancés looked at each other. Lonnie nodded his head. Sara knew what the nod was about. She asked *his* great-grandfather about the house he grew up in.

"Well, our family lived in New Orleans then. Our house was what we called a shotgun house. Small. Long and narrow—like the barrel of a shotgun. No hallways. One room opens into the next. First you walk into the living room. Then you go into the middle rooms—two of them. We had a large family. We used them as bedrooms. In the back was the kitchen."

"So, in order to get into the kitchen you had to go through the bedrooms? Even company had to do that? Isn't that … a little too personal for strangers to be in your bedroom?"

"Company never came into the kitchen. Just stayed in the front room. The kitchen was the hottest place in the house. Who wanted to be in the kitchen unless you had to? It gets pretty hot in New Orleans a good part of the year. You want to be in front—away from the kitchen."

After dinner the couple was alone. They talked once again about the apartments they had seen. This time their conversation had a new dimension. They both realized that their ideas about "home" had been formed a couple of generations before they even came along. The needs they were trying to fill were not just their needs, but their great-grandparents' needs as well. Without knowing it, Sara and Lonnie were standing for others from their background: family members with experiences rooted in different geographical regions.

Dealing with Identity Groups

As we will see in Chapter 7, differences in culture, family, profession, and even lifestyle can give rise to conflict, without our necessarily being aware of it. For the engaged couple above, the revelation of their families' influence had the effect of restoring resonance. Each could begin to understand the other's reasons for rejecting their choice of apartments.

In most cases, it will be less obvious when identity groups influence our conflicts. Most of us have a long list of groups we identify with, and understanding their influence on our underlying needs is an enormous task. Gayle has listed some of her identity groups below:

> Women, African Americans, mothers, people over forty, single people, college graduates, consultants, entrepreneurs, peacemakers, short people, walkers, drivers, people who have a place to live, Atlantans, New Yorkers, Brooklynites, urbanites, credit card holders, wine lovers, meditators, world travelers, book lovers, book writers, television viewers, meat eaters, ex-cigarette

smokers, divorced people, working moms, single moms, working women, music lovers, choir members, the Burnett-LeGall family.

At any point in time, one of these groups may influence a decision that Gayle is making or give rise to a need within her. Recognizing our identity groups can help us when conflicts arise based on group affiliations that differ from those of our conflict partner.

℘ Exercise: Identity Groups

In Chapter 1, we focused on awareness of our own needs. This exercise is designed to increase your awareness of the influences that arise from your identity groups. In your peacework journal, list all of the groups with whom you identify. For the next week, continue to jot down a group whenever you think of it.

At the end of the week, review your list. Can you think of a time when being a part of any one of those groups gave rise to a new conflict or added fuel to one already in existence? Reflect on how you might have acted differently during the conflict if at the time you had been aware of the influence of your identity group on your actions and reactions.

Historical Inequities in Conflict

Identity groups often have histories. If we are a member of an identity group that historically has been either mistreated or privileged, that history can affect how we react in a conflict. Certain kinds of conflicts contain within them the elements of historical inequity, potentially causing a present-day conflict to be bigger than just what's happening right now between me and you; it is also between "my people" and "your people."

On her way home from an out-of-state client meeting, Gayle hailed a taxi at the airport. As she was riding through the Upper West Side of Manhattan, she got a call from home asking her to pick up some disposable diapers for her then one-year-old daughter. It was pretty late, and most of the stores uptown, where she lived, were closed. She had just enough cash to pay the taxi driver and give him a tip. With her stress level slightly elevated, she asked the driver to stop at the next drugstore. She ran into the store, grabbed a bag of diapers from the shelf, and took it to the cash register. Knowing she didn't have enough cash to pay for the diapers, she reached into her wallet and took out her credit card, asking the white cashier if the store accepted credit cards.

He smiled at her and said, "Sure, as long as it's yours."

"Excuse me, of course it's mine," she snapped at him.

"What happened to your sense of humor?" he said.

"I don't think it's funny when people assume my credit card is stolen."

"Wait a minute. Wait a minute. I didn't say that."

"That's what it sounded like to me."

"Lady, I've been making that joke to people all day. Usually people laugh."

Gayle was a little surprised. She wasn't sure how to respond. The man seemed both kind and genuinely confused by her response. "Okay, look, I get asked that question a lot. It's just that...well, people are always assuming that black folk like me are doing something illegal. I'm always asked to show ID, and I get the third degree when I use my credit cards or write checks. It sounded to me like you were just doing the same thing."

"Well, I'm sorry," he said. "I really didn't think...well, it was just a joke. I was surprised when you didn't laugh. Please accept my apology."

"It's okay. I'm stressed. I shouldn't have snapped at you."

"You live and learn."

"Yes, you do."

You do. They did. In that situation they took the time to listen and talk to each other, so they both came away from the experience feeling like something good had happened.

The conflict between those two strangers was not just between a cashier and a customer. They were both standing for centuries of historical inequities between blacks and whites. The history of their identity groups clashed without any deliberate forethought on the part of the two individuals involved. All of a sudden they were in conflict, having to find their way to some understanding. In this case, they did.

Scenes like this are often the source of rapidly escalating conflict, because the feelings behind the inequities are intense. The inequities are historical, but also remain very present in contemporary society. Gayle didn't know whether the cashier was being deliberately racist when he made a remark about credit cards. The cashier lacked the awareness to know that a remark like that coming from a white man carried with it centuries of oppression. However, both of them remained open with the other and dialogued about it on the spot. That helped.

Dealing with Historical Inequities

When approaching a conflict that brings with it historical elements such as these, it can be helpful to sort out the past from the present by thinking about the following questions:

* What is the power relationship between the parties involved in the present conflict?

  The cashier was in a position of power, since he could accept or reject the credit card.

* To what extent does this conflict reflect a history of inequities?

  Historically, economic discrimination against blacks has sometimes taken the form of assuming that all black people are dishonest.

* Is that inequity actually present in this conflict?

  The white cashier could have been making that assumption, but he said he wasn't. There was something in his manner that allowed Gayle to believe him.

● Does this conflict contain "ghosts" of that history that cause either or both parties to jump to conclusions?

This particular conflict was all about the "ghosts" of racism. Gayle initially jumped to the conclusion that the white cashier's remark was racially motivated.

● Does the inequity continue to be rooted in the attitudes of the people involved in the current conflict—that is, do prejudice and a power imbalance still exist?

Racist behaviors and remarks still happen, so it was possible that prejudice and racism were actually underlying the present conflict. However, Gayle, with the help of the cashier, finally decided that he was not being racist—that, in this particular conflict, prejudice was not present.

This chapter shows how conflict can involve others who may not even be present. It may involve historical family, cultural, or racial constituents. One or both parties in the conflict may be unaware of the powerful role these constituencies play in the current situation. By becoming aware of and acknowledging influential elements in our lives, such as our identity groups and other constituencies, we gain greater insight into the forces of conflict at work all around us. Conflicts that bring with them elements like racial or cultural tensions are often highly charged and can escalate quickly. Chapter 7 provides a number of steps that you can follow to better understand the cultural influences you bring to a conflict and help you avoid escalation.

Our willingness to hang in there when faced with a conflict can be a pivotal decision. It is not always possible to explore the motivations behind other people's actions. But when we take the time to reflect on such motives in ourselves—to explore what lies behind our own behavior—we may discover that alternative strategies for conflict resolution can be pursued. Sometimes, peace can come from simply taking the time to understand how our differences can contribute to the discord between us.

CHAPTER 7

꿏

Is the Conflict Really About What Happened?

Ms. Peach told Mr. Crown that there was something wrong with Ms. Kravitz. When Ms. Peach walked into Ms. Kravitz's classroom to return some markers she'd borrowed earlier that day, Ms. Kravitz screamed at her to get out. She did this in front of all the students. How humiliating!

Later that day, Ms. Kravitz told Mr. Crown that Ms. Peach had barged into her classroom and disrupted her lesson with some complaint about dry markers. When she politely asked Ms. Peach if they could talk about it later, Ms. Peach stomped out of the room. "She's so nuts," Ms. Kravitz complained.

Mr. Crown wondered what had really happened. Part of him wished he'd been a fly on the wall during those disputed three minutes so he could see what had really taken place. If he had actually been there, his story about what happened might differ from both of his colleagues' stories, but would it have been the truth? There were twenty-eight fourth-graders who witnessed the incident. If they each were interviewed separately, we might hear twenty-eight different versions of the story.

How can you tell what *really* happened in a conflict? You can't. We each view the world through our own set of filters. These filters determine our point of view in a conflict. They are a combination of many factors, including:

- *The events we actually notice.* We don't notice everything. Much of what occurs in any situation escapes our attention.

- *How we interpret the events.* Our interpretations are informed by our past experiences; our constituencies (visible and invisible) and identity groups; our geographic, economic, and cultural backgrounds; our current mood; and many other factors.

- *What we remember about the events we noticed.* We can recall our interpretation of an interaction with greater ease than we can its actual details. We also remember the events that are most important to us, because they set off meaningful associations from our own past or present circumstances.

When resolving conflict, attempting to find out what really happened can be frustrating. Keep in mind that each person has her or his own point of view about what happened. Each point of view has validity. To resolve the conflict, the important task is to discover a way to meet each person's underlying needs. Ms. Kravitz's story about what happened may reveal her underlying needs. Likewise, Ms. Peach's story might reveal *her* unique needs. In hearing each other's stories, their best approach would be to search for needs rather than "truth."

Cultural Filters

As we saw in the preceding chapter, a person's cultural background is a major factor in shaping the filter or lens through which he or she views the world. All people in all cultures experience the same basic needs and feelings. Those are the universals among us. However, we each view the world and express our needs and feelings differently. We learn how to express ourselves from those who raised us—from our parents, our extended family, our community.

Different cultures express themselves in different ways. We send and receive messages not just through spoken language, but also through nonverbal communication.

When we think about culture, we commonly think about the aspects of culture that we can see and that we are all conscious of: music, arts, cuisine, dress, celebrations, and religions. However, the aspect of culture that influences how we relate to people on a daily basis is generally less easily observable at first. It is this aspect of culture that we absorb as we grow, even in our preverbal years. We very often lack conscious awareness of the worldview, beliefs, and mode of expression that we developed as young children. We do things and react to events largely by habit. We don't know why we do what we do. We just do it.

Sheila was born, raised, and lived most of her adult life in New York. She eventually relocated to New Orleans, where she'd visited quite often. As a visitor, she had come into contact with New Orleans culture—the music, the arts, the celebrations, the food— all of which she found very exciting. However, once Sheila moved to New Orleans, she came in contact with aspects of New Orleans's deep culture she had not fully experienced before.

The first encounter that made her aware of some of the differences between the cultures of New York and New Orleans occurred when she called a cab. The dispatcher said the cab would come in ten minutes. Ten minutes came and went. No cab. Sheila called again. Once more she was told "ten minutes." An hour later there was still no cab. She called again. The dispatcher explained that Sheila had called for a cab while school was letting out and all the cabs were in use. Plausible, but why was she told ten minutes? The dispatcher had no explanation for this—just a subtle note of exasperation in his voice.

This situation happened over and over until she reflected on the deep cultural differences in assumptions that were buried in the interaction. The assumptions that guide us are not explicit or even conscious most of the time. It is rare for somebody to be able to articulate the deep assumptions he or she is making, but nevertheless they determine our behavior.

First, there was a difference in assumption about time. In New York, ten minutes means ten minutes. New Yorkers embrace a more precise attitude about time. If you make a commitment to be somewhere within a particular time frame, the assumption is that you will get there close to that time, even if it means moving heaven and earth to get there. If you are late, you are being irresponsible and rude. In New Orleans, on the other hand, there is an assumption that heaven and earth have their own time frames. Many things can intervene that might make you late. These are often more important than the commitment to a particular time.

Second, there was a difference in assumption concerning "the word." In New York, a lot of information is conveyed through language. You say what you mean and you mean what you say. Given Sheila's cultural frame of reference, it was reasonable for her to expect that the dispatcher really meant ten minutes. In New Orleans, however, "the word" is only a small portion of how information is conveyed. A person is expected to take time to observe all the circumstances that could possibly influence an event. That unspoken knowledge about all the environmental factors is assumed, so when the dispatcher gave his standard answer, "ten minutes," he expected that the person receiving the information would also know that this was a stock response for which he was not completely accountable. He assumed Sheila knew that if she called during a busy time, there would be no way she could get a cab for another hour or so.

The first few times this happened Sheila got very angry at the dispatcher, but doing so failed to get her a cab any sooner. Eventually, as she learned the city's habits, she stopped calling during those times when cabs were unlikely to be available.

Deep Culture and Conflict

The same set of cultural differences affected Sheila's personal life when she was a newcomer to New Orleans. In New York, everyone she knew carried calendars or planners that guided their lives. If you made an appointment, either for work or to see a friend, both

parties wrote the appointment in their calendars. Generally, bar-
ring illness or another emergency, people kept their appointment.
When Sheila first moved to New Orleans, her friends sometimes
failed to keep the appointments they made with her. When this
happened she would get angry at what she assumed was irresponsible or disrespectful treatment. She began to feel that her friends
were not really her friends—that their behavior meant they didn't
really want to see her.

All of this was projection on Sheila's part. That is, she was projecting her own assumptions onto her friends. If she had cancelled
or failed to show up a number of times, she might, according to
her New York assumptions, be sending a nonverbal message that
meant, "You are not important." She believed her New Orleans
friends were sending such a message. She attributed *her* assumptions about behavior to them without first recognizing that they
had a different set of assumptions and interpretations about
appointments and friendship. If Sheila had chosen to confront
them without a fuller cultural understanding, she might have
caused unnecessary and confusing conflict. Instead, she decided
to assume that cultural differences existed that she might not yet
understand. She allowed herself a period of time to observe the
people around her before making any final judgments.

Eventually she came to understand that those whom she
believed to be her friends really were her friends. They demonstrated that to her in many ways—by supporting her dreams, by
comforting her through her disappointments, by dropping everything in an emergency to come to her aid when she needed it.
Sheila no longer expected that a plan made with a friend would
always occur in the time, place, and manner in which they had discussed. She ceased to get angry at a "no show" or cancellation of
an appointment. She chose to reserve her confrontations for com-
mitments that were truly important to her. For example, when a
friend borrowed her car for "an hour" and came back four hours
later, Sheila expressed her anger. Her friend had known that she
had no food in the house and was hungry. Sheila told her friend up

front that she needed the car to go shopping for groceries. It wasn't the first time her friend had borrowed the car; in fact, she did so frequently to run errands. This time her friend had stopped for a few hours to visit with her mother after running her errand.

Sheila was able to address the situation without the extra baggage of assuming that her friend didn't care about her. There was no hidden hurt in Sheila's voice and none of the rage that would normally accompany hurt. She could say plainly, "I needed the car back sooner, and I've been hungry all afternoon. Next time please get the car back to me right after you run your errand, or if you plan to make another stop, call me to check if I need the car right away." Her friend responded with, "Okay, I'm sorry." Since then, Sheila's friend has generally followed through on her promise to come right back or call first.

Dealing with Cultural Differences

Cultural differences that are not understood or acknowledged can make a conflict worse, causing the individuals involved to get wrapped up in their interpretations and assumptions about the incident rather than focusing on their underlying needs. Remember that cultural differences can be big and loaded, such as race and religion, but they also can be subtle, such as the filters through which we view the world based on our family of origin's communication style. The following steps, developed by Inter-Change Consultants, an East Coast firm specializing in leadership development and strategic diversity management, can be useful in dealing with conflicts that may turn out to be culturally related:

1. **Be aware.**

   To any conflict situation, bring an awareness that deep, unspoken cultural differences may be operating.

2. **Pause.**

   Pause before you react. Working through the exercises presented in Chapter 3 can help with this step.

3. Describe.

Center yourself with the exercises in Chapter 3. Then, taking your time, begin to observe the interaction. Describe to yourself what really happened as accurately as you can, with as little embellishment as possible. Focus on information gained through your five senses. (For example, "She agreed to return the car in an hour. She returned it in four hours.")

4. Connect your needs and feelings.

Focus first on yourself to maintain your balance and center. Ask yourself what you are feeling as a result of the behavior that initiated the conflict. Remember: Try not to get caught up in past cultural conflicts. (If your feelings are so strong that you cannot separate the past from the present, return to step 2.) Then assess what your needs are in the current situation. (For example, "I need to have my car available to me so that I can buy food"—a survival need.)

5. Hold back your interpretations.

As you turn your attention to your conflict partner, separate your interpretations from your description. Don't jump to conclusions. (When Sheila's friend failed to return her car in an hour, her initial interpretation was "She doesn't care about me. She's being disrespectful.") Know that your interpretation is only your theory about a person's motivations. Like any theory, it may be right, but it also may be wrong. Bear in mind that we have a tendency to move to interpretation very quickly and to remember our interpretations more strongly than our descriptions.

6. Refrain from evaluations.

Refrain from judging the other person as right or wrong, good or bad. Most often, our interpretations are accompanied by a judgment about the person. Frequently, the judgment is negative. (For example, "She is an irresponsible and disrespectful person.") Unchecked interpretations and evaluations between people from different backgrounds (and that's all of us, since we each bring our own cultural filters to every interaction) can give rise to stereotyping and prejudice. Suspend your evaluation.

7. **Gather information.**

   Become informed about deep cultural differences between you and the other person through a combination of observation and information. Observe yourself (another skill discussed in Chapter 3); come to know your own assumptions about the meaning of different behaviors. Refrain from projecting your assumptions onto the other person.

8. **React appropriately to the situation.**

   When in conflict, address your grievances in a way that is free of the baggage and loaded emotions often produced by culturally based misinterpretations.

9. **Work to find a solution that meets each party's underlying needs.**

   Express the needs you have that are most relevant to the actual situation at hand. Inquire about the other person's needs. Express a desire to help the other person meet their needs. (Communication skills that will facilitate these last two steps are the topic of Part III of this book.)

ಞಞ

We perceive the world through the lens of our cultural upbringing. Our most basic beliefs are shaped before we have any awareness that there are many others in the world who perceive things differently and whose cultures give them very different information about the ways to behave.

In order to successfully navigate through the layers of cultural perception inherent in many conflicts, the skills of observation and self-awareness are critical resources. From there, the keys to resolution lie in accepting the differences in others while knowing and understanding our own preferences and needs.

CHAPTER 8

❧

Is the Conflict About Something in the Past?

Early in their relationship, Marcus and Gina had a falling out. Gina went out with an old boyfriend and only told Marcus about it after the date. However, Marcus had first heard about it through the grapevine, which caused a big blowup between them. Although they were able to make up and get back together, the incident planted a seed of distrust in Marcus's mind. Distrust turned to jealousy, which grew through the years. Gina had a circle of friends with whom she occasionally went out to dinner and a movie. These social occasions with friends, in particular, became a source of tension between Marcus and Gina.

One day, years later, Marcus's cousin told Marcus that he'd seen Gina out with another man. Marcus confronted Gina. Gina denied it. She said she had been faithful since the incident years before. She said that Marcus's cousin must be mistaken, or else just causing trouble. Marcus didn't believe her. He began to question her in great detail on a regular basis about where she went and who she was with, causing more conflicts between them. The tension between them grew. Gina reacted by retaliating in her own way: by criticizing Marcus's style of dress and his messy habits.

Marcus shot back, "Why do you have to wear those low-cut blouses? You need to change your clothes."

"You liked how I dressed when we first went out."

"Well, I don't like it now!"

Gina refused to change clothes. The conflict escalated. They screamed and yelled—all about the blouse. Marcus stomped out. The next day, Gina told her girlfriend that they broke up because Marcus was trying to tell her what to wear. To the friend, that did not seem like a good reason to break off a relationship. However, there were underlying issues of trust and possessiveness. Marcus and Gina were fighting about more than just the blouse. If Marcus had traced the argument back to its source, he might have realized he was still fighting about Gina's date with her old boyfriend many years before. For him, it was not about the present conflict; it was about an unresolved conflict with Gina from the past.

For Gina, too, the conflict was about the past, in two ways. First, Marcus's tendency to question Gina about her activities and associations reminded her of her father. She loved her dad dearly, but he had been strict about regulating his daughters' activities. That left Gina and her sisters feeling very restricted and often resentful. He was less restrictive with his sons. Second, Gina's previous boyfriend also had had a tendency to act jealous and possessive when she went out with friends, but he did not restrict his own social gatherings with his male friends. Gina was having a conflict with Marcus about the cut of her blouse, but the "ghosts" present in the conflict for Gina were her relationships with her father and her ex-boyfriend, that is, her previous experiences with jealousy and restrictiveness.

Ghosts from the Past

It would have been helpful if Marcus and Gina could have paused, taken a few minutes to cool down and center themselves, and then asked themselves the following question: Is this conflict about what just happened between us, or is it about something that happened many years ago? It is not unusual for an incident to set off an inappropriately severe reaction. Instead of fighting about the present situation, without knowing it we may be bringing the "ghosts" of our personal history into the conflict. Such ghosts might include

- our history with this particular person

- our history with this kind of conflict

- our history with a person with similar characteristics from our past.

Elements of all of these kinds of ghosts were present in the conflict between Marcus and Gina. In addition, they were grappling with ghosts from society's past. It was not only their personal histories that affected their interaction, but the long history of the world in which they lived. The last century has been one of conflict and change concerning the redefinition of gender roles. Often conflicts between men and women reflect the long history of those gender relationships, a history that reaches back several thousand years.

Anthropological evidence supports the claim that many of the pre-Biblical societies in the region of the Fertile Crescent were matriarchal in nature. That is, inheritance and family identification were passed down through the mother's lineage. As scholars point out, determining the identity of a child's mother was easy and therefore practical. However, over a period of time patriarchal societies conquered the matriarchal societies. In a patriarchal society, family identification and inheritance is determined through the father's lineage. Since determining the identity of a child's father was more difficult, issues arose involving female fidelity and the necessity to restrict the interactions of women with other men. (This topic is explored in detail in *When God Was a Woman*, by Merlin Stone.)

In a sense, you could say that Gina and Marcus were fighting a battle that is thousands of years old but still going on: the battle over the gender-based double standard in attitudes toward sexuality. As illustrated in Chapter 6, many of our interpersonal conflicts can be traced to historical struggles. We frequently find ourselves fighting the world's battles within the microcosm of our everyday relationships.

Core Issues

For most of us, particular issues exist that seem to set off especially strong emotions during conflict. These issues may seem to repeat themselves throughout our lives. They emerge in conflicts with a number of different people again and again. We may find ourselves fighting the same battle over and over, but in a different time, in a different setting, and with different people. The issues that trigger these recurring battles could be thought of as our *core issues*.

Certain phrases tend to signal the presence of a core issue:

"I've heard this before."

"All my life I've been fighting to…"

"You're just like my mother and my ex-wife. They both wanted me to…"

"Everywhere I go I have to deal with people who…"

"Why don't people just let me live my life the way I want to and stop…"

Each person has a different set of core issues. Donny was always dealing with people who were disappointed with his accomplishments and wanted him to work harder. George was always feeling isolated from other men because he wasn't into sports. Julia kept running into people who tried to "boss her around" (as she described it). Susan consistently felt that her accomplishments were overlooked. Gina seemed to get into conflicts with the men in her life about restricting her interactions with others.

We all have one or more core issues we are dealing with. When one emerges, it carries with it the sum total of all our struggles and frustrations from times past when the issue emerged. We are fighting about more than just the conflict at hand with this person right now. We are fighting about all the accumulated ghosts from the past that the core issue brings with it.

Dealing with Ghosts

Returning to the present can be a major challenge when a conflict has many layers from the past attached to it. Doing so requires a willingness to be an observer of yourself. First, notice that your emotions are running high. You may be showing early signs of the fight-or-flight response, or you may detect the presence of an increase in tension that could lead to fight or flight. Pause. Cool down. Change your body's physiology. Find your center (all skills described in Chapter 3). Be ready to think about the conflict with a more rational mind.

Second, ask yourself the following several questions to determine if any ghosts from the past are influencing the conflict:

- Does this person remind me in any way of someone from my past?

- Does this conflict remind me in any way of a prior conflict I've had with this person?

- Does this issue remind me in any way of an issue I've dealt with before?

If the answers to any of these questions are yes, you may need to revisit the past in order to return to the present conflict and resolve it.

If an issue from the past has not been cleared up and is present between two people in conflict, it may be necessary to revisit the issue. If possible, enlist the aid of a third party (a mediator, counselor, therapist, member of the clergy, etc.) to help the two of you revisit sensitive subjects and work through unresolved issues. Unresolved issues may need to be explored so that the emotional charge around them can be released, permitting you to resolve the conflict at hand without additional baggage.

If the issue is something from your own past (say, the person reminds you of someone from your past, or the issue is one you've encountered before in your interactions with others), you may need to explore the issue on your own or with the help of a counselor or therapist. You may need to resolve your feelings about the person(s) from your past. You may need to come to an understanding of issues that arise repeatedly in order to realize their significance and develop a strategy for dealing with them as they arise. This is a long-term approach.

In the short run, you may need to recognize that a particular conflict is about more than the present moment. It's about the past as well. Try to detach yourself from the intense emotions that the past carries with it and see the present conflict as clearly as you can. Use the steps spelled out in Chapter 7 to describe to yourself what really happened with *this* particular person, in *this* particular conflict. Try to discover the underlying needs that exist right now and come up with a solution that satisfies the present circumstances.

We are complex beings, and therefore we are prone to conflict. What appears as a simple gesture, remark, or behavior on the part of another can signal the beginning of fight or flight for us. Our past comes screaming into the present, filling us with emotion and sending us into patterns of response that fail to help resolve the situation and often exacerbate it.

Dealing with the current conflict requires that we employ the skills of self-awareness and self-observation that have become so critical to understanding our needs. The deeper challenge is to explore the past, to resolve those old and often painful patterns that continue to show up in our present lives, to successfully resolve our long-term issues, and to put old ghosts to rest.

CHAPTER 9

ℒ

How Can We Bring the Conflict Back into the Present?

Two people were alone in a room eating dinner. One said, "Pass the salt." The other passed it. The first salted her food. The two people didn't talk to each other for six months afterward. What happened?

Let's use what we learned from the preceding chapters to take a closer look at this incident. Then we'll close Part II with a review of the steps involved in bringing a conflict back to the present.

Now we return to the salt-shaker saga.

The description (what was observable with the five senses):
Jane and Susan, sisters, are sitting at Jane's kitchen table eating the dinner that Jane cooked for them. Susan says, "Pass the salt."

Jane pinches her mouth and squinches her eyebrows. She points to the salt-shaker, which is midway between them, and then reaches for it.

Susan also reaches for the salt-shaker and grasps it. With large and swift motions, she shakes salt all over her food.

Jane's interpretation:

"We were eating dinner. I had tried so hard to cook a meal Susan would like. I'm always trying to please her in some way, and it never works. She always acts like such a princess. A seventy-three-year-old princess, ha! Our parents, may they rest in peace, spoiled her rotten, and she still acts like the world revolves around her. But, I try. Believe me, I try.

"You know, she's never supported me in my attempts to care for my health. Those of us with heart conditions are always up against the rest of the world, people who like everything over-salted, fried, and fatty as hell. Nobody ever seems to want to accommodate any health concerns. My ex-husband, may he rest in peace, ignored all his doctor's recommendations, and now I have to visit him in Montifiore cemetery.

"Well, Susan, she just grabbed that saltshaker. Didn't even stop to taste the food, and I seasoned it with all sorts of herbs and spices to make salting unnecessary. What an insult! She doesn't even trust me or trust my cooking."

Susan's interpretation:

"My sister Jane! What a piece of work! She disapproves of everything I do. My God, a simple phrase like 'Pass the salt,' and she gets an attitude. Like I'm a degenerate indulging in all sorts of debauchery. Of all the silly things: salty eating. She has never approved of me or my friends. She won't spend a minute with any of them. She refused to come to my party yesterday. She calls my friends 'that artsy bunch.' What does she mean by that? I can still remember when she refused to dance at my fifteenth-birthday party. She's never changed. She disapproved of me then, and she still does now. Well, I've had enough. That's the last time I'll give up an evening for her. The last time!"

The outcome:

Susan and Jane finished dinner quietly. Susan left right after dinner. The next time they saw or spoke to each other was six months later—at Thanksgiving dinner, cooked by their sister-in-law.

What Were They Really Fighting About?

The above fictional anecdote opened with the phrase "Two people were alone in a room." However, were Jane and Susan really alone? Was their conflict really about what happened in this incident, right there and then, between the two of them? Let's see.

Is the conflict really about this incident?
The saltshaker episode was one event in a recently escalating conflict between the sisters. We know Susan was upset because Jane didn't come to her party the day before. That resulted in hurt and resentment on Susan's part and primed the pump for emotional hijacking. There may have been other incidents in the chain of escalation that we don't know about.

Is the conflict only between us?
Jane was "standing for" all people with health problems. Susan was "standing for" her friends.

Is the conflict really about what happened?
Both Jane and Susan immediately jumped to conclusions about what was happening. Instead of using the language of the five senses (description) to talk about the incident, they moved directly to their assumptions and interpretations. Susan's interpretation was that Jane disapproved of her request for salt. Jane's interpretation was that Susan was being unsupportive of her attempts at healthy cooking, that Susan had insulted Jane's cooking by not tasting before salting, and that Susan did not trust her.

These were all theories the two sisters espoused about why the other said or did particular things. They each embraced their own theories as absolute facts without speaking to the other about them. No wonder they refused to communicate with each other for six months.

Is the conflict about something in the past?
The past was very much in the present. Susan and Jane both were playing out ancient sibling jealousies relating to their parents' attention to and treatment of them. Susan still carried resentment

for an incident that occurred when she was fifteen. Jane still carried resentment from her past history with other individuals, including her deceased husband, who had not taken his heart condition seriously enough to be careful about diet. Susan resented Jane's past attitude toward her friends. And on and on.

Two People Alone in a Room?

Two people are *never* alone together in a room, just having a conflict about the present situation. We carry the past with us, and we carry with us all the people and situations that influence us.

Conflict is complex. It has many layers, like an onion. Getting through those layers to the heart of the matter is a little like peeling an onion. It stings our eyes and sometimes makes us cry. Its taste is sharp, but it's nourishing. The sweetest part is in the center. The center is the present, the "here and now," the "you and me." If we can work out what is happening between us in the present moment and negotiate a solution that keeps a peaceful future in mind, then we stand a chance of creating peace in our everyday relationships.

Returning to the Present

Let's review the steps involved in bringing a conflict back to the present.

Observe

Become an observer of yourself (review Chapter 3).

Become an observer of others (review Chapter 4).

Become Familiar with Your Triggers

Know what triggers fight or flight in you (review Chapter 2).

Notice the cues that indicate you may be overreacting—the physiological, mental, and emotional cues that lead to fight or flight (review Chapters 2 and 3).

Pause (review Chapters 2 and 3).

Cool down and get centered (review Chapter 3).

Reflect

Ask yourself the following:

What's really happening?

- Describe, using data obtained from observing the events with your five senses.

- Connect to your own feelings and needs in the present. Focus on yourself first.

- Refrain from interpreting the motives of others.

- Refrain from judging or evaluating the other person.

Is the conflict about this particular incident?

- Is it a link in a chain of escalation?

- What else is this incident about?

- How did the chain get started?

- What were my needs then?

- What do I really need right now?

Is the conflict between you and me?

- Are there others we are standing for (visible or invisible constituencies)?

- What are their needs?

- Are my needs and my constituencies' needs the same?

- What are my needs?

Is it about the here and now?

- Is a hidden "ghost" from the past influencing the conflict?

- Is there something about my past with this person that I need to clear up?

● What did I need then?

● Is my own history with others influencing my feelings and interpretations? What past issues do I need to work through?

● What are my real needs now?

The goal of this internal dialogue is to keep you grounded in the present moment as much as possible, to free you from the emotional hijacking that other influences can trigger, and to help you get clear about your own needs. Notice that every line of questioning comes back to the issue of identifying your real (underlying) needs. If you can be clear about your real needs, you are that much closer to resolution.

As Part II has shown, what appear to be simple words exchanged between two people alone in a room can turn into fodder for another round of conflict. We can use the process of closely examining our conflicts to help us understand the conflict's origins and the reasons behind our emotional reactions. When we ask ourselves critical questions about the observed behavior of others, about our own behavior and feelings, and about our past history with the elements of the conflict, we begin to gain valuable insight. The use of internal dialogue to dissect our conflicts allows us to take the necessary steps back, to reflect, observe, and become present to our current feelings, needs, and emotional state.

Part III

❧❧

Engaging the Other Person as a Conflict-Solving Partner

CHAPTER 10

ℰ℀

Transforming the Relationship Through Communication

The real work of creating peace is never done alone. As we discovered in Parts I and II, clarity about your needs, your feelings, your past, and your behavior in a conflict is important. Equally important are the needs and feelings of the other person. Even in a conflict between strangers, we can ask, are both people satisfied with the result? Have their needs been met? But it is not enough to figure out all the answers in our own minds. We must engage the other person to change our relationship with them.

As we saw in earlier chapters, resonance between people in conflict transforms their relationship from an adversarial one to a partnership seeking resolution. Developing the skills to bring resonance to a conflict is the focus of Part III.

To create peace in our relationships, we must act as partners in a complex dance, observing, describing, and revealing ourselves. We must be focused in our efforts to gain understanding of each other, and at some point, we must do it together, whether face to face, phone to phone, or through instant messaging. This requires communication skills we are rarely taught, but ones that we certainly need in order to be successful in our relationships. In this chapter, we will focus on developing those skills.

The Communication Potential

Felix: Oscar! Oscar! I can't believe it. You are a complete slob.

Oscar: Watch the way you talk to me, you little....

Felix: Your cigar ashes are all over the place. Everywhere I go in this living room I see a mess you've made.

Oscar: My ashes will stay right where they are.

Felix: It's bad enough that you keep your own room like a pigsty, but I told you I was having a dinner party tonight. My guest will be here soon. Clean up, now!!

Oscar: Felix, you've got a stick up your.... That prissy little proper lady you're bringing over will be enriched by the ashes of a real man's cigar!

Felix: What you need is to deal with your obsession with that phony symbol of manhood you wave in the air.

Oscar: What you need is to get that broad in your bedroom. Now leave me alone.

(Curtain drops. Audience applauds.)

That was a hypothetical scene from an old but familiar situation comedy. The audience applauds because we all laugh at the antics of fictional characters. It is not our problem, so we can see the humor in their struggle. Sometimes we laugh because they're acting out a familiar problem, and watching it onstage helps us to see the humor in our own struggles. However, if you or I were involved in a roommate relationship like that of Oscar and Felix, we might want to talk to each other in a different way in order to make our lives together more peaceful...and more feasible.

Communication is the process of sending and receiving messages. In the child's game known as Telephone, a speaker whispers a message into a child's ear, who then whispers it into the next child's ear, and so on until the message is passed to the last person in the group, the receiver. The receiver says out loud what he/she heard. Generally, the message the receiver reports is much different from the original speaker's message. The game is a metaphor for interrupted communication. The speaker sends a message that gets interfered with in many ways; the end result is that the receiver hears something entirely different from what was sent. The message intended is not the message received.

When resolving a conflict, there is much information that needs to be communicated:

- what each person wants (their positions);

- each person's underlying needs;

- an explanation of each person's positions and needs, to enable the other person to understand;

- some indication that each person understands what the other is saying;

- alternative suggestions for meeting the underlying needs;

- solutions agreed to by both, including details about how to carry out the solutions.

If communication is successful, the process results in a resolved conflict. If communication is unsuccessful, the conflict can escalate. In addition, a successful communication can result in more than just the peaceful resolution of the conflict; it can also bring about positive transformation in the relationship.

We all share a universal desire to be heard, recognized, acknowledged, and accepted. The transformative potential of successful communication lies in meeting that universal need. Sometimes just the feeling that we are being heard calms us down and brings us to a state of willingness to look for solutions. Our negative feelings about the listener may dissipate, and we move a little bit closer to forming a bond with her or him.

We form bonds with others when we can recognize something about ourselves in them—when a feeling of resonance is created. Creating resonance is one of the goals of successful communication. We achieve resonance through communication when we are able to express ourselves in a way that enables the other person to recognize our needs or feelings as similar to something he or she may have experienced; when we are able to listen carefully enough to really hear and understand what the other is saying; and when we are able to listen carefully enough to hear both the unique and the universal qualities of the other person's message. Resonance transforms not only the conflict at hand, but also the relationship.

Oscar and Felix had a conflict over the state of the living room. Felix wanted Oscar to clean up after himself. He had a guest coming for dinner. His underlying need was to set an atmosphere that he felt would impress the guest. He needed Oscar's cooperation. He didn't get it. He began his communication by yelling at Oscar and calling him names. That closed communication down completely. Oscar got stubborn and called Felix names. Soon they were having a put-down match. Somewhere in the course of the dialogue Felix did express what his need was, but by then Oscar didn't care. He was not open to hearing it or to finding ways to meet Felix's needs. Felix had shut down the communication between them in his first sentence. The message intended was not received. Neither person felt heard, recognized, acknowledged, or accepted. This scene was one more episode in the antics that resulted in the deterioration of their relationship.

What Closes Down Communication?

Blocks to communication can occur while a person is either receiving or sending a message.

Receiving Blocks

Receiving blocks (behaviors on the part of the *listener* that block communication) include

- interrupting the speaker
- changing the subject
- looking away and tending to other tasks

- not focusing attention on the speaker

- listening with a focus on planning your response

- using facial expressions and body language that indicate a lack of attention or respect for the speaker

These behaviors convey to the speaker that what he is saying is unimportant and that the listener is uninterested in hearing or understanding it. When the speaker feels he is not being listened to, he is likely to stop trying to communicate—to shut down in some way. (See Chapter 11 for a detailed discussion of how to listen in such a way as to promote effective communication.)

Sending Blocks

Sending blocks (behaviors on the part of the *speaker* that block communication) include the following (among others):

- judging ("You're such a slob")

- diagnosing ("You need to deal with your obsession with that symbol of manhood")

- criticizing ("It's bad enough that you keep your own room like a pigsty")

- condescending ("That prissy little proper lady you're bringing over")

- preaching ("You would be a much happier individual if you would put some order in your life")

- retorting ("My cigar ashes will stay where they are")

- not indicating understanding ("Whatever...")

- avoidance (not sending a message at all)

Each of these sending blocks closes down communication by putting the listener on the defensive. If the listener feels she needs to defend herself, then she is busy thinking up her defense or counterattack instead of focusing her attention on the speaker's message. She is still in combat mode and therefore is not listening with an open mind focused toward finding solutions. (See Chapter 12 to learn how to convey your message in such a way as to promote peaceful conflict resolution.)

Divisive Communication

A third kind of block, *divisive communication*, causes the people involved in a conflict to feel as though they are far apart from each other and that resolution seems hopeless. It ultimately has the impact of closing down communication, but the modes of expression are subtler than those described above. We will therefore explain each in more detail. Divisive communication behaviors include the following:

Counterposing

Counterposing involves stating your position in such a way that it seems like your position and the other person's position are opposites and can't exist together.

For example, Felix needs Oscar to clean up his stuff before the dinner guest arrives. He might say, "Your chaos makes it impossible to share space with you." Oscar might counter with, "Your compulsive need for order is driving me nuts."

Both Felix and Oscar used counterposing statements in that exchange. Felix and Oscar *do* have opposite tendencies when it comes to chaos and order, and the comic thread in their story lies in the conflicts that arise from their attempts to balance these two elements. However, the relationship is about the process of gaining that balance. Stating their tendencies as incompatible drives the two roommates further apart. That's counterposing. Counterposing in the middle of a conflict distracts from a possible solution to the conflict at hand.

A more unifying approach would be to name the forces that feel incompatible at the moment, and to do so in a way that could lead to a solution. Felix might simply ask Oscar to help clean up. Later, he might bring up the larger issue by saying, "I seem to need a lot more order in the household than you do. What can we do to make it so that we both feel comfortable?" We will talk more about creating the "we" in Chapter 13.

Polarizing

Polarizing is describing small differences in position in extreme terms so that the differences seem larger than they are.

Felix and Oscar might be discussing how to approach the landlord about fixing a loud bang in the pipes. The landlord is reticent to fix anything. Oscar wants to call the landlord and demand that it get fixed. Felix advocates a subtler approach, involving inviting the landlord to dinner so that he can hear the bang for himself. A polarizing conversation such as the following might ensue:

> *Oscar:* Felix, you never want to confront any problem.
>
> *Felix:* You just want to completely destroy any relationship we have with the landlord by threatening him.

Neither Oscar nor Felix is accurately describing the other's approach to the problem. Instead of discussing the pros and cons of each idea, they are characterizing the other's idea in the extreme, thereby making their respective approaches seem incompatible. They are refusing to create a common ground upon which the two ideas can be joined.

Using nonnegotiable differences in worldviews to divide

Ellen Raider and Susan Coleman, in their collaborative-skills training, talk about worldview as an element in any negotiation. They theorize that we each have a unique worldview, which results in our attitudes, beliefs, and values. Our worldview comes from our personality, culture, and life experience. The more deeply we hold our worldview, the more likely we are to see it as nonnegotiable. In resolving conflict, we need to understand and respect the other party's worldview. We need to try to resolve conflict by discovering basic underlying needs instead of challenging each other's worldviews.

Sometimes worldviews clash with each other and are incompatible. Some conflicts can result from a clash in worldviews. However, we often get caught in the mistake of blaming the conflict on a clash in worldviews when resolution could more easily be achieved if we instead focused our discussion on finding solutions to underlying needs.

For example, there are many instances in the relationship between Felix and Oscar when the following discussion might occur:

> *Oscar:* Felix, you are too compulsive for me. I just don't feel life should be lived that way. Spontaneity is the spice of life!

> *Felix:* I am a person who appreciates beauty. The chaos you create destroys that beauty for me.

Here, they are stating their differences in worldview. Despite those differences, there may be many reasons why the relationship should continue, many reasons to resolve the conflicts that arise. If every conflict were stated in terms of worldview differences, no solutions would be possible. Each conflict should be negotiated on its own terms; each attempt at resolution should address the particular set of needs underlying the conflict at hand. (That's basically the message of Part II of this book: how to get past differences in worldview and other mindsets and return to a focus on current underlying needs.) Felix and Oscar could still keep in mind the differences between their worldviews. In an attempt to find solutions, however, those differences need to be respected and accounted for, not used to divide them further. The household routines they agree on might have to include both Felix's desire for order and Oscar's desire for spontaneity.

Cultural Differences in Communication Styles

In Chapter 7 we discussed how differences in culture affect conflict. In particular, communication is greatly impacted by differences in culture. We communicate with each other through words, gestures, body language, tone of voice, and facial expression. Every aspect of these modes of expression is originally learned from those who raised us—from our cultures. Although cultural differences provide many opportunities to enhance our lives, the differences can also create a communication challenge.

Blocks to successful communication can result from misunder-
stood cultural differences, so that the meaning of the sender's
message is not received as intended.

Anthropologist Edward Hall identified several aspects of differences among cultures, including communication styles. He
talks about cultures as having a characteristic he calls *context*.
Context consists of the sum total of everything that surrounds an
individual—family, community, environment, climate, geography,
history, and so on. Certain cultures are high in context, others are
low in context, and still others are in between. This delineation
refers to the degree to which context is taken into account in
determining a person's worldview and habits of expression.

In *high-context cultures* the meaning of a communication is
derived from a great many of these environmental factors and
from looking at the various modes of communication, both verbal
and nonverbal. Furthermore, in determining what a particular
message means, other contextual factors are taken into account,
such as the status of the communicators, their family backgrounds, the personal history of the people involved, and the situation at hand. In a *low-context culture*, all that information is nice
to know, but the actual words spoken are attended to more than
anything else.

Recall the example in Chapter 7 about Sheila's attempts to
call a cab in New Orleans. The cab driver consistently told her that
the cab would arrive in ten minutes, words she took literally. Her
low-context assumption was that because he said "ten minutes,"
he meant that in roughly six hundred seconds her taxi would
arrive. However, his high-context assumptions were that Sheila
knew about all the environmental factors involved in delivering on
that promise, and that she would figure out on her own that "ten
minutes" was simply an indication that some time would pass
before her taxi arrived.

Cultures that are lower in context tend to be rooted in West-
ern civilization, have colder climates, are more urban, are more
industrialized, and have a higher per capita education. Cultures
that are higher in context tend to be more rural or agrarian, have

warmer climates, and are rooted in African, Asian, or indigenous American cultures. These statements reflect tendencies rather than strict categories, and significant exceptions exist to these generalizations.

The following chart, developed by Inter-Change Consultants, summarizes the differences in communication styles between high-context and low-context cultures:

Communication Styles

HIGH-CONTEXT CULTURES	LOW-CONTEXT CULTURES
High nonverbal focus Voice tone, facial expression, gestures, and eye expression carry significant parts of the conversation.	***Low nonverbal focus*** Message is carried more by words than by nonverbal means.
Message implicit Verbal message is a result of context (i.e., situation, participants, nonverbal cues). The form of the message and its information will be filtered accordingly.	***Message explicit*** Verbal message is based upon information to be conveyed; preference is for precision and concise language; context is less important.
Indirect One talks around the point and embellishes it.	***Direct*** One spells things out exactly, using tools like bulleted text or thirty-second sound bites.
Message is art form Communication is seen as an art form, a way of engaging the person. Stories are told, rich with detail.	***Message is literal*** Communication is seen as a way of exchanging information, ideas, and opinions in concrete terms.
Disagreement personalized One is sensitive to conflict, which can have lasting effects. Conflict is often avoided or referred to a third party because it is so disharmonious.	***Disagreement depersonalized*** People deal one-on-one with the conflict and get on with the task. Focus is on rational solutions rather than personal ones.

When dealing with cultural differences in communication styles, it is important to keep in mind the potential for misreading a communication even if the words are clear to you. Consider taking extra time to clarify what the person means. If you are in conflict with a person, allow for the possibility of misunderstanding. Don't jump to conclusions about what the other person means. The message one person intended may not be the same as the message the other person thought he or she received. Recall the interchange in Chapter 6 between Gayle and the store clerk. Had Gayle stuck with her first assumptions about what the store clerk was intending to communicate, the misunderstanding would have remained in place, and both people would likely have left the scene feeling insulted and angry. Instead, Gayle allowed for the possibility that she had initially misinterpreted the store clerk's meaning. The situation was resolved with both individuals feeling good about the exchange.

The Choice to Communicate

Remember that the decision to resolve conflict (or not to resolve it) is a choice. It is the same with communication. Sometimes we consciously make the simple choice to communicate, and other times we're unaware that we're making such a choice. Communication is often one of those things we do "naturally," without thinking. Cultural and other differences can cause us to choose not to communicate, or not to communicate at the deeper level of needs.

In the film *Changing Lanes*, Ben Affleck and Samuel L. Jackson play men whose lives intersect because of a car accident. Though neither is hurt physically, throughout the movie they inflict damage on one another's lives. In the initial exchange between the two men, we can see in their communication the result of their differences in race, class, profession, and age. Doyle Gibson (Jackson), an African American insurance agent around age forty-five, wants to exchange the appropriate information so that the problem can be handled in a formal manner. Gavin

Baneck (Affleck), a white, fast-track Wall Street lawyer around age thirty, feels his time is too important to waste on the details. There is nothing in the two men's outward appearance or initial interaction to suggest that they have any commonalities, any room to find common ground. Each man is caught in his own frame of reference, unable to see the other with compassion, and their lack of compassion foments escalating tension and abusive behavior on both sides.

Eventually, after doing as much damage as they can to one another, Baneck and Gibson begin to acknowledge one another's humanity. Once they make that acknowledgement, the quality of their communication changes. They are able to speak to one another about the forces in their lives that brought them to the scene of the accident and propelled them into the dangerous spiral that followed. They engage in open communication and shift their relationship, settling their dispute and moving on with their lives.

Communication is the most powerful tool we have for creating peaceful relationships. How we engage the other party in the communication process will have significant impact upon our success in resolving any conflict. Acknowledging that cultural differences may cause others to embrace ways of communicating and worldviews that are different from ours is an important step in communicating successfully. Maintaining an awareness of when we are blocking communication, as either the listener or the receiver of a message, is essential to keeping the process of resolution on the right track. Once we've done so, we can transform our listening and speaking behaviors into ones that open communication and move us toward peace.

℘ Exercise: Effective Communication

1. Bring to mind an example from a book, movie, play, or TV show of a conflict in which the parties involved fail to reach a win-win solution, either because of culturally influenced differences in communication styles, or because one or

both parties engage in communication-blocking behaviors. (Daytime soap operas are terrific sources for examples of ineffective communication styles. Reality TV is full of scenes involving misunderstanding and miscommunication. The plots of classical operas are often built around culturally based communication difficulties.) Alternatively, create your own scene, either fictional or based on a real-life experience.

2. In your peacework journal, rewrite the script, creating a new ending in which a win-win resolution is reached because at some point in the course of the conflict, the warring parties shift how they're communicating. Have fun with your rewrite. Be imaginative. (Can you imagine Hamlet and Ophelia exploring their underlying needs in Shakespearean English? Or Tupac and Biggie Smalls talking through the differences in their needs?)

3. For the next two days, pay attention to the communication blockers you hear around you. Try to identify their types from the list provided earlier in the chapter. You can do this part of the exercise anywhere—at work, at school, or while watching television.

4. Do you use communication blockers? After you have completed step 3, spend one day listening for communication blockers as you speak. If you use any (and most of us do at least some of the time), think about how you could have expressed yourself without using blockers. In your peacework journal, write down the blockers you used, and then give two examples for each blocker of how you could have communicated more effectively.

CHAPTER 11

ℰ

Creating an Opening by Listening

In the previous chapter we looked closely at some of the blocks to communication, including the blocks created by poor listening. In contrast, careful listening, also called *active listening*, has the potential for creating a way to both heal the conflict and improve the relationship.

The Goals of Active Listening

The goals of active listening are

- to understand and acknowledge what the speaker is saying;
- to understand and acknowledge the needs, feelings, and concerns of the speaker; and
- to diffuse the intensity of both people's difficult feelings.

A scene between two friends who meet in a restaurant illustrates the potential of active listening:

Carmen (in a high-pitched voice): Girl, I have been sitting here waiting for you for over an hour!

Lucinda: Sorry I'm late. I got caught in traffic. (Lucinda takes her coat off and hangs it over the back of the chair. She sits down at the table across from Carmen and picks up the menu.)

Carmen: That's your standard excuse. (Lucinda puts down the menu and looks across the table at Carmen. Her facial expression shows concern.) I've been sitting here in this restaurant waiting for you like a fool. I should have left a long time ago.

Lucinda: Look, I didn't mean to leave you sitting here like that. Were you embarrassed having to wait that long?

Carmen: Well, yes, but that wasn't the biggest part, really. (Lucinda nods her head.) It's just that I cut out from work early to get here on time, raced around like a maniac, and you seem to have taken your time.

Lucinda: So, you're upset because you went out of your way to get here for me, and you feel I didn't do the same for you?

Carmen: Yes. (Sighs audibly.)

Lucinda: Carmen, I was thinking about you waiting all that time while I was tied up in traffic. I know you can't stand it when people are late. It's like being on time means I'm respecting our friendship.

Carmen: Right. That's it.

Lucinda: You've never said anything to me before, but do you always get pissed off when I'm late?

Carmen and Lucinda continued discussing the issue of punctuality, but now Carmen was calm and feeling positive about Lucinda once more. She felt heard and understood by Lucinda, and that took the emotional edge off the discussion. Because Lucinda stopped explaining her lateness and started listening, she was able to hear Carmen—loud and clear. She understood, maybe for the first time, what being on time meant to Carmen—that it was more than the clock; that it had something to do with feeling that they both respected each other and their friendship. Lucinda heard Carmen's underlying needs.

How to Listen Actively

Let's look at the components of active listening. We can do this by examining in closer detail what Lucinda did in her interaction with Carmen.

1. **Give the speaker your full attention.**

   Lucinda put down the menu, faced Carmen, and looked directly at her. Making eye contact while listening can help you focus on the speaker, and can help the speaker know that you are listening. However, eye contact is not necessarily comfortable for all people. In some cultures, eye contact is inappropriate between two people of different status. We recommend doing what feels natural to you, while being sensitive to whether it is also comfortable for the other person. Whether or not you make eye contact, orient your body so that you are facing each other rather than facing away. Eliminate any other distractions. Don't tie your shoelaces, organize the papers on your desk, look for the cell phone, or any of the other numerous tasks that might require part of your attention.

2. **Remain centered and calm, even in the face of someone else's anger.**

   Carmen was angry with Lucinda and began the conversation by expressing that anger. Lucinda remained calmed and listened to Carmen, even in the face of Carmen's anger. If you are listening to someone who is angry at you, it is possible that a remark he or she makes will set off an emotional response inside you and you will be tempted to either strike back or avoid the situation. Breathe deeply (though subtly), find your center (which you've been practicing doing, based on the exercises in Chapter 3), and commit yourself to listening before responding.

3. Try to understand what the speaker is saying.

Lucinda stopped explaining *her* situation and started listening to what Carmen was saying. Focus your mental energy on both hearing the words the other is speaking and understanding the message as fully as you can. *This is how resonance begins.*

4. Resist mentally digressing into your own agenda.

Lucinda did not prepare a defensive answer, think about similar incidents in her own life, give Carmen advice, or use what Carmen was saying to confirm her own negative fears about Carmen's reaction. She shut all that out of her mind, including the list of things she had to get done by tomorrow, and just listened to Carmen. The listener's (Lucinda's) attention was on the speaker (Carmen). This does not mean that the listener will never have an opportunity to express her own concerns. It means that during that moment of listening, the listener puts her own personal thoughts or agenda aside and gives the speaker the gift of her undivided attention.

5. Show your concern with your body language, tone of voice, and facial expression.

Nonverbal modes of communication convey a lot. It's hard to describe what concern looks like for every individual. If you are genuinely concerned it will show. In Lucinda's case, she nodded. Concern also appeared on her face.

6. Paraphrase the essence of what is being said.

Lucinda paraphrased Carmen's communication. To paraphrase, repeat the main idea or essence of the speaker's concerns in your own words. Let it flow naturally with the dialogue. Paraphrasing helps you check your own understanding about what the speaker is saying. If you are wrong, the speaker will no doubt say so and generally will explain once again. Also, a paraphrase lets the speaker know that you do understand, or at least that you are trying to understand.

7. **Name or identify the other person's needs and feelings as well as you understand them.**

   For example, "Are you upset because...?" and "I know that being on time means something important to you. It's like being on time means I'm respecting our friendship." This is a step toward finding solutions. It is one way of discovering the other person's underlying needs and feelings. Also, just the act of naming a feeling often creates an emotional shift—a release of tension around that feeling. It is this emotional shift that is the beginning of the conflict-solving partnership, for now the other person knows that you are connected to them by your willingness to understand. If you name their need or feeling incorrectly, ask the other person to clarify, if they haven't done so. Let them know that you are trying to understand.

8. **Use questions and probes to bring out more information about the speaker's views, needs, and feelings.**

   For example, "Have you gotten angry in the past when...?" "What did you want to have happen, instead of...?" Be sensitive about your questions. Avoid cross-examining. Clarify.

9. **Listen with an open heart.**

   Even if you hear things that shock or surprise you, try to remain in a listening mode. Remind yourself that the speaker is someone whom you are trying to understand, and refocus your attention on her or his feelings and needs. Listening with an open heart requires accepting (though not necessarily agreeing with) what you hear and, by extension, accepting the other person.

Listening as a Healing Tool

Listening is a powerful healing tool. Of all the skills for healing and conflict-resolution we have acquired over the years, active listening is one of the most effective for healing a wide range of ills in many different contexts. As our experience attests, if someone comes to you one-on-one to talk about a situation that troubles them, most of the time active listening will calm them and help them see through the maze of disturbing thoughts. It will bring them to some sort of internal resolution.

We all have a powerful need to be understood. Sometimes we don't understand ourselves. Active listening has the power to help us understand ourselves and to help us feel understood by another. It does this by acting as an auditory mirror.

Sometimes when a person presents us with a problem, our tendency is to want to "fix" it. We feel we have to offer advice or analysis. However, most of the time people don't take the advice that is given them. They often resist or resent the analysis. The most powerful lessons we learn are the lessons we teach ourselves. An active listener helps us learn *for* ourselves, *from* ourselves.

Occasionally people *do* take our advice or learn from an analysis we offer. That generally happens when the advice or analysis closely mirrors their own understanding of the situation. As with all learning, people gain understanding of themselves and others if the information is presented at their level of readiness. Active listening helps the listener discover that level.

The power of listening with an open heart is expressed by the following simple passage, from Margaret Wheatley's book *Turning to One Another*: "We have the opportunity many times a day, every day, to be the one who listens to others, curious rather than certain. But the greatest benefit of all is that listening moves us closer. When we listen with less judgment, we always develop better relationship with each other. It's not the differences that divide us. It's our judgments about each other that do. Curiosity and good listening bring us back together."

We can use active listening to build a bridge of understanding across the gulf of conflict that divides us. Active listening permits us to gain a clearer picture of how we differ from one another, without allowing the new information to further divide us. The next piece of the puzzle lies in being mindful of the way we communicate our own needs and beliefs. That topic is addressed in the next chapter.

᭒ Exercise: Active Listening

In order to effectively use active listening skills in the midst of a conflict, you will need to practice them frequently. These are not skills that we tend to use in our day-to-day activities (though we would probably benefit from using them). The exercise below can be used at any time to practice active listening.

1. Ask a friend or colleague (one whom you are *not* in conflict with) to work with you. Tell them you are going to practice your listening skills and you need their help.

2. Have them describe a *positive* life-changing event or situation. Ask them to describe the event with some detail, including their feelings at the time it happened.

3. Using the steps outlined in this chapter, focus on the speaker, paraphrase, reflect their feelings, and ask questions to gain more information. Remember that if you incorrectly reflect a feeling or paraphrase a thought and they correct you, that's okay. The correction gives you better information than you had before. (The first few times you do this you may feel awkward, so remember that you are learning something new. In time you will be able to use this type of listening with relative ease.)

4. The conversation should last for about ten or fifteen minutes. You should be able to summarize for the speaker, in a few sentences, the event and its overall impact on his or her life.

5. After you summarize, ask the speaker if they felt you were really listening to them. Have them tell you if they thought you missed any important information or feelings. Make sure to write their feedback in your peacework journal.

After you've done this exercise a few times, incorporate the feedback you've received and start to use your skills in everyday situations, with your friends, spouse or partner, coworkers, and children. In your journal, keep track of any positive results you have from active listening. See if changing the way you listen makes a difference in your relationships. Then, when you feel you are ready, begin to use the skills when you are having a conflict.

CHAPTER 12

ℰℒ

Clearly Communicating Your Needs and Feelings

The listening skills described in the last chapter are designed to enable the "receiver" of the message (i.e., the listener) to hear and understand what is being said regardless of the manner in which the message is sent. If the listener is able to stay centered and calm and to retain the active listening focus, much can be accomplished to promote understanding. We are talking about a skilled listener who is able to stay constant in the intention to resolve conflict whether or not the speaker is also a skilled conflict resolver. However, situations do arise that can throw even a skilled listener off center. More discussion will be devoted to such circumstances in later chapters.

Now let's focus on the sender. Let's examine what is involved in the skill of sending a message so that there is a greater chance of being heard by the listener, even if the listener is not a centered, focused conflict resolver. The emphasis for the speaker is on taking responsibility for delivering her or his message in a clear, non-threatening way. This skill is called *assertive informing*.

141

The Goals of Assertive Informing

The goals of assertive informing are

- to provide information about the speaker's own needs, concerns, and feelings;

- to avoid putting the listener on the defensive, instigating a "counterattack" or chasing the listener away;

- to provide information in such a way that it has a chance of being heard and taken seriously by the other person.

Consider the following dialogue:

Wilma: How can you stand to listen to this? Would you turn it off?

Walter: Why should we turn it off? Because you don't like it? I like to listen to this disc jockey.

Wilma: Look, I'm driving. It's too much noise.

Walter: Why do you have to manipulate everything?

Wilma: Why do you think you always need to get your way? Right now it's my nerves that are important.

Walter: Oh s—t. Can you just stop it? Just stop.

Wilma: I'll stop when you shut the radio off.

Both characters' modes of communication were attacking and demanding. Each stated what he or she wanted inflexibly and in harsh tones. The other person responded in kind. Here's an alternative way to conduct the same dialogue:

Wilma: Walter, please turn that radio show off. That disc jockey's voice is loud and jarring. It's snowing and I really need to stay calm and to concentrate on my driving. His voice is making me feel more jumpy. Can we find another station that is more soothing?

Walter: I know it's messy out here and you need to concentrate on the road. I just really like this disc jockey. I've been an avid fan of his for years. I listen to him every chance I get. Today he's sponsoring a contest for tickets to the oldies concert at the Dome next weekend. As soon as he gives the clue I'm going to call in on my cell phone.

The differences between these two dialogues are numerous. This first was destructive. In a destructive dialogue parties often state their positions inflexibly, without going deeper to underlying needs. Instead, their messages justify their positions. In the first dialogue both Wilma and Walter stated their positions as demands, adding a phrase or two to justify their demands, like "I like to listen to this disc jockey" or "It's too noisy." In both of these justifications there was no reference to the underlying need.

In a destructive dialogue the parties verbally attack each other in order to strengthen their positions. Walter and Wilma used insults like "Why do you want to manipulate everything?" and "Why do you always need to get your way?" These are attacks, even though they are disguised as questions.

How to Get Your Message Across Assertively

The steps involved in assertively communicating what you want to say include the following:

1. **State your position flexibly, and move quickly to a discussion of underlying needs.**

   In the second dialogue Wilma opened by doing just that. Her position was to turn off the radio. Her underlying need was to remain calm while driving. She spent time explaining the underlying need behind her request to turn the radio show off. Walter acknowledged her need (he displayed good active listening) and then provided some information about why he wanted to listen to the disc jockey (he wanted to enter the contest). They each said their piece in a flexible manner, remaining open, friendly, and generous in attitude toward the other.

2. **Be clear about your needs, and be willing to communicate them.**

Although you are communicating in a friendly and generous way, do not desert your own needs. Do your best to identify what your underlying needs are in the situation at hand, and communicate them as clearly as you can. Assertive informing involves standing up for your own needs without destroying or undermining the other person.

3. **Be aware that tone of voice and body language play major roles in sending a message that is received as friendly.**

Assertive language delivered with an aggressive tone of voice can be interpreted as an attack, causing defensiveness and hostility. Although you could not "hear" the tones of voice used by Wilma and Walter in each dialogue, in the first dialogue their tones were short, sharp, and hostile. In the second dialogue their tones were softer; they each used a friendlier and more melodic voice. In any discussion about tone of voice, we need to remember that tone of voice in a dialogue can't really be rehearsed. How you sound has a lot to do with your intent. If you are feeling friendly toward the other person, what you say will come out in a friendly tone. If you are feeling hostile, your voice will sound hostile even if you try to sound friendly. Therefore, part of checking your tone of voice involves checking your attitude. Enter the dialogue with a generous and caring attitude toward the other person—caring about them, caring about yourself, caring to be received positively, and caring to hear the other person.

4. **Refrain from jumping to conclusions about the other person's intent.**

As discussed in Chapter 10, cultural differences exist in both verbal and nonverbal messages. Variations exist in the subtle meanings of the words used, body language, and tone of voice. For this reason, it is important to refrain from jumping to conclusions about a person's intent. Sometimes, due to cultural differences, a message that is intended to be friendly and conciliatory may be received as hostile and aggressive—and vice versa.

Pause before you decide you are certain about what the other person meant and act on it. Give them the benefit of the doubt. Stay calm and centered and open to resolution. Engaging in open dialogue with the other person about personal or cultural differences in communication style can help you understand their intent. It can also help you understand the different meanings of certain words and actions when delivered in different contexts.

Addressing Grievances: "I" Messages

You share a driveway with your neighbor. He consistently parks off the paved driveway and on your lawn, leaving tire tracks on the carefully maintained strip of grass next to the driveway. You have a grievance you want to express. How do you do it without declaring war or creating a hostile situation with your neighbor?

Attempt to inform your neighbor about what you are feeling, what you needed in the past, and what you need now. Be specific about the events without being accusatory.

Use neutral language like, "It's frustrating to me to see tire tracks on the lawn after I've put effort into seeding it and caring for it. It's important to me to have a smooth, green lawn. I like how it looks."

An attack would be, "You keep messing up my lawn!"

This is not an easy thing to do. It's important to use your own words. It's also important to remain positive while trying to address the situation as clearly as you can. If you intend your message to be positive, it will come out as positive. If you are misinterpreted, use that as an opportunity for clarification.

Be sure to express yourself in a way that's consistent with your cultural norms. For example, if you come from a culture in which it is inappropriate to express strong feelings, then honor that. If "angry" is too strong a word for how you feel, then use a less aggressive term. Conversely, if you come from a background in which people commonly use strong language with each other, then using a word such as "concerned" to describe how you are feeling may feel out of place.

With active listening the focus is completely on the other person—the speaker. If you are the active listener, you need to remind yourself that the moment of listening is not about you, the listener; it's about the other person. In contrast, with assertive informing the focus is on the speaker. If you are the speaker, the one who is raising the grievance, you may need to remind yourself to keep your focus on you rather than on the other person. For that reason, this form of expression is sometimes called an "I" *message.*

An "I" message is about

* how I feel;

* what I need and why; and

* how the situation impacts my life.

A "you" message

* is about the other person's characteristics, and

* attacks and accuses and has the potential to hurt, destroy, or put the other person on the defensive.

Even a relatively mild "you" message such as "You're driving carelessly" has a tendency to put the listener on the defensive. When you attack, the listener's response is often to counterattack, be on the defensive, or avoid the situation. Whatever their reaction, the listener is no longer listening, but rather worrying about their own response and planning their next move. The listener is no longer open to exploring solutions.

With an "I" message, the intent is not to hurt or destroy in any way. The intent is to inform another party about yourself in a way that has the possibility of being heard.

The "I" message can be broken down into several components. Below, we provide a formula that involves each component.

However, the formula is not meant to be used verbatim. The purpose for learning such a formula is to understand what goes into an "I" message. Ultimately, in order to be effective, you must put the "I" message into your own words. It must be part of your own natural way of expressing yourself. Here's the formula:

I feel _____
(name the feeling)

when you _____
(describe the specific behavior or situation that is at issue)

because _____
(describe the impact the behavior or situation has on your life)

and I need _____.
(name your underlying need)

In the case of the driveway scenario, an "I" message would be:

I feel frustrated

when you leave tire tracks on my lawn

because I like the lawn to be smooth and green, and it makes extra work for me

and I need some help with keeping this area green.

Again, it's important that, rather than trying to follow the formula verbatim, you understand the intention of an "I" message and use your understanding as a guide to speaking. If you simply use the formula without understanding it, it would be easy to turn an "I" message" into a "you" message. For example:

I feel that you are taking advantage of my good nature

when you drive so carelessly that you mess up my lawn

because you never seem to care about my feelings

and I need you to stop that.

There's an accusation in every component of the latter message. It's a "you" message from start to finish.

An "I" message is *not* a magical formula. It is designed to keep communication open and to avoid instigating further problems, and often it accomplishes these things. However, despite all your care in constructing the perfect "I" message, the situation may be so volatile that your wonderful "I" message causes an explosion anyway. The next few chapters will give you additional communication skills to help bring you closer to resolution and to deal with explosive situations.

℘ Exercise: "I" Messages

Below are two scenarios, each followed by good examples of "I" messages. Read the scenario, and then write your own "I" message in response to the scenario. *Once you have done that,* compare what you've written to the sample "I" message that's presented below the scenario. When you state an "I" message in your own words, it may read differently from the "I" messages included here. Keep in mind that it is unimportant whether your wording matches the wording contained in the example. What is important is to be clear and assertive in your intent—that is, to avoid masking a "you" message in the language of an "I" message.

> *Scenario*: Your boss approaches you about taking on another project. You've been working very hard and are feeling a bit overwhelmed right now.
>
> *Sample "I" message*:
>
> **I feel** concerned
>
> **when you** ask me to take on this project
>
> **because** I've been working very hard on the other projects
>
> **and I need** more time to do a thorough job on them before starting the next.

Scenario: Your roommate (spouse, sibling, child, parent, etc.) has borrowed your favorite pen and used up the ink without replacing it.

Sample "I" message:

I feel upset

when you use up the ink in my pen

because I do a lot of writing

and I need a pen that writes smoothly like that one.

Now think of a real grievance from your life—a scenario from either your past or your present. Practice writing an "I" message to the other person involved in the conflict. It may take several revisions before you settle on wording that feels comfortable to you. Once you've written an "I" message that you like, read it back to yourself to make sure it is clear and that you have avoided hiding "you" messages in it. Consider using the "I" message to initiate a discussion with the other person about the situation.

CHAPTER 13

༔

Creating the "We"

In the last two chapters we discussed a particular kind of dialogue in which the energy flows as follows:

"A" speaks ──► "B" listens (the focus is on A)

then

"B" speaks ──► "A" listens (the focus is on B)

You can think of this flow in terms of who gets the attention: first "A" (whoever initiates the discussion), then "B." For the conversation to have a positive outcome, there must be a give and take of attention through which each person gets the opportunity to share their needs with the other, and each person hears the needs of the other.

In this chapter we will turn the focus away from "you" or "me" and place it on "we."

Mediation: Becoming Partners in Solving a Problem

Sheila is sitting in the airport on the way to a mediation in which she is one of the disputants. She is engaging in this process because she feels she has been "wronged" by an organization she

worked for. She has chosen mediation as an alternative to litigation. Litigation is a time-consuming and costly alternative. The
goal of litigation is to prove the other party wrong and to "damage" the other party. The process entails each party attacking the
other in an aggressive fashion. A third party decides who is right
and who is wrong—and who is awarded the "damages." Litigation
is about them versus me and me versus them. The two parties are
adversaries in a contest in which someone else will decide their
fate. Never during the process do the two join together in solving
the problem they share: the conflict that erupted between them.

In mediation, by contrast, it is necessary for the disagreeing
parties to join together as partners. This is because the mediator
does not decide the outcome; the two parties do. The mediator, a
neutral third party, facilitates the process in an impartial way. It is
therefore necessary for the two "opposing" parties to become partners in the process of resolving conflict.

Sometimes litigation is the best alternative, and Sheila
intends to move to litigation if this mediation is not successful. In
her experience as a mediator, she has found that although mediation is successful in a large majority of cases, sometimes the parties fail to come to an agreement that suits them both.

In preparing for this day, Sheila has made extensive notes for
herself about what she wants to say. However, while working on
this chapter about creating the "we," she realizes that her notes
are full of "you" messages; they're all about what the other party
did. They contain attacks, accusations, and attempts to place
blame. If she and the other party go to court, they will need to
establish blame. The party who is to blame will lose. However, in
win-win conflict resolution, placing blame is beside the point. The
point is to find a resolution that meets the needs of both parties.

It is important to Sheila during the mediation to go into the
details of the events that led up to this point. She realizes she
must ask herself why she wants to talk about all of that. It was a
conflict that became an out-of-control escalatory spiral, and
dredging up the details is confusing and painful. However, a voice
inside Sheila wants to dredge it all up, partly to prove she is not to

blame—to defend herself—but mostly because she is very angry. In fact, she is enraged, and she needs to express it. Above all, she needs to feel understood.

It is difficult to think about a partnership with the other party, difficult to imagine unity with them, to imagine becoming "we" when a person is sitting on unexpressed anger. However, in most conflict scenarios a partnership existed before the conflict began. The partnership may have been fleeting—for example, a grocer and a customer can be in a short-term partnership around a purchase of apples. The partnership may have been long-term—a work relationship, a friendship, a love relationship, a family relationship, etc. Even if the partnership does not resume in the same form it took before the conflict, the disputants are partners for the moment—partners in solving a problem.

What Makes a Mediation Successful?

Two mediations from Gayle's work stand out in her memory: one successful, the other abysmal. They illustrate how and why a mediation can go well, and how and why it can go poorly.

The successful one was a mediation conducted by several high school students whom she had trained as peer mediators. The students were in the second year of a mediation program established by their school because of a sharp increase in verbal and physical violence among the students. The events that led to the mediation started early one morning in March, when the buses were just pulling up to school. That morning, the buses that carried students from two rival housing projects arrived simultaneously. The teenagers from Worthington Homes disembarked at the same time as the kids from Percy Court. A girl from Worthington walked over to a young man from Percy and smiled. She said, "You are too fine, you and me need to get together." He looked at her without appreciation and said, "Naw, I don't think so. You ain't what I'm trying to get with."

That was at 7:50 A.M. By 8:30 it was all over school that Worthington Homes and Percy Court were going to war. Three of the school's student mediators, Jamal, Quintavious, and Salmera, went to their mediation coach (a parent who was also trained in mediation) and told her they wanted to mediate the disputants. The coach was reluctant, but she agreed that if they could convince the school counselor to authorize the mediation, she would work with them. It took the students and the school until 10:30 A.M. to decide to proceed with the mediation. And it was a very risky decision. Not only might war between the two groups break out anyway, but if the mediation failed, the fight could ignite on school grounds, fueled by a mediation that was ultimately sanctioned by the principal.

By 11:00 A.M., forty-three students, six of them mediators, and the two adults responsible for the mediation program were sequestered in the peer mediation room, where they remained for the rest of the school day.

The mediators, by all accounts, were brilliant from the very beginning. They displayed their skills by maintaining objectivity and building the trust of those in conflict. They stuck to the rules of mediation: no name-calling; focus on the problem(s); one person talks at a time; each disputant looks at and addresses the mediators instead of the other disputants; each disputant speaks from their own experience by saying "I" instead of "we" or "you" when expressing feelings. The mediators listened to what was said and, equally important, to what was not being said. They asked questions for purposes of clarification and to surface additional information. As a result, it came out that although the girl from Worthington insisted that she had been disrespected by the boy from Percy, a skillful mediator, through gentle probing, was able to get her to admit that she had a beef with a girl in her algebra class who she knew liked the boy, and talking to him was just a way to get back at this other girl.

The other students present were there because they were the ones who might take the dispute into violence no matter what was settled between the two initial disputants. Worthington Homes and Percy Courts had a long history of conflicts, and these young people would fight if it wasn't clear that the conflict was resolved.

Over the course of the four-hour mediation, many voices were heard. Past disputes were brought up and resolved. A facilitated dialogue took place between the rivals, and a tenuous peace was won.

For the rest of that school year, no further violence occurred between Worthington and Percy. Furthermore, the use of the school's peer mediation program increased by 230 percent. It was a successful mediation for everyone involved.

A year later, Gayle was asked to mediate a dispute for the same school system, this time involving adults. Gayle was assured that both of the parties had agreed to the mediation and were willing to work toward resolution. What unfolded, however, was a mediation that was almost guaranteed to fail.

The parties present were the assistant principal and the counselor of a middle school, and the parents of one of the school's students. Gayle partnered with a member of the central office's staff who was also a trained mediator and a colleague.

Within the first twenty minutes it became clear that one of the parties, the school representatives, had not come to resolve the dispute. They had, in fact, been told to attend the mediation by their management as a step to avoid litigation. They were resentful of the process and were only going through the motions. A break was called at this disclosure, and Gayle requested their genuine participation, giving them the option to end the mediation. They assured Gayle (though she remained doubtful) that they were sincere in their efforts toward resolution, so the mediation continued.

The parents told their story calmly, painting a picture of a school that disliked their child and disliked them and systematically worked to damage the family. The school officials painted the parents as unreasonable and often irrational in their dealings with the school. At each layer of the story, the mediators searched for points of common interest that might be used when the process shifted to the solution phase. Each party appeared to genuinely want what was best for the student involved, though they had very different ideas about how that could be accomplished.

Gayle's mediation partner began to move the process toward looking for solutions, although Gayle's gut told her it was too early. She checked in with the disputants, asking if they felt ready to look for solutions, or if they thought there was more to the conflict that needed to be explored. To Gayle's surprise, everyone agreed that they should move forward. If she regrets anything, it was not taking a stronger stand to continue exploring the dispute.

So the parties began to search for solutions. Yet every time they were close to agreement, the parents began to tell another layer of the story. The events they spoke about provided further proof, from their perspective, that the school had treated them unfairly. During the second break Gayle asked her mediation partner if they could extend the mediation to two or three meetings, but she was told there was no budget to pay her for additional time. When she agreed to do it at no cost, she was told that it was unlikely the school officials could be released for any additional time. And so, two and a half hours into the mediation, it became very clear that the best they would do was to patch up a bad situation, but it would remain unresolved.

Even with this understanding, Gayle was unprepared for what happened next. As the parties were reaching what appeared to be an agreement, the mother started to shake her head. Gayle asked her what part of the agreement she was having a problem with, but she remained silent. She just continued to shake her head. One of the school officials rolled her eyes. By now, the mother's shoulders were starting to shake and tears were beginning to fall. Her husband said in a very soft voice, "She is crying because our oldest son is dead."

And so the parents' real story began to unfold. The dispute had not begun with the child they were discussing, or with this school, or even with these administrators. It had started eighteen months earlier when their oldest son, who had been home-schooled with his brothers and sisters, asked his parents to let him attend the local high school. Initially they would not allow him to go, but he was persistent; eventually he even begged. Finally the parents agreed, but with strong reservations. They enrolled him in the school. Almost immediately, other students began to pick on him and he was isolated. His appearance (he wore thick glasses and different clothing) and the fact that he was Muslim, ate different foods, and did not know any of his classmates very well all worked against his being included in the students' social hierarchy.

From the story told by the parents, the child was relentlessly harassed and abused by fellow students. Administrators of the school told the parents they were unaware of the level of isolation he suffered. He took his own life before the school year ended. His suicide changed his parents' lives and the lives of his classmates forever.

His classmates held a memorial service for him at the high school. They wrote his parents letters of sorrow. They learned what on some level they'd known all along: that their behavior had caused him a pain of such great magnitude that he could not live with it. Had the students allowed him to coexist with them peacefully, mediators would not have been called in a year and a half later to mediate an irresolvable conflict involving his younger brother.

What the parents needed could not be provided through the mediation that had been arranged. For one thing, some of the parties to the conflict were absent. A successful mediation would have required representatives from the eldest brother's high school and also, more than likely, from the school district's central office. And though the parents ultimately sought damages in a court of law, it is unlikely that their wound could be healed by money.

Mediation is a powerful tool for uniting parties who are unable to work through a conflict on their own. In order for a mediation to have a positive outcome, several necessary elements must be present from the outset:

1. All the parties must have a willingness to resolve their conflict.

2. All the constituencies, or their representatives, must be present.

3. The mediators must be trusted by the disputants to create and maintain a safe environment for communication during the process of mediation.

4. The mediators must at no time take sides.

5. The process of communication must be used to unite the parties.

6. The focus of the communication must remain on gaining understanding.

Mediation is being used more and more often to avoid the financial and emotional costs of going to trial. In divorce, child custody disputes, and workplace disagreements mediation has become an accepted practice. Local family courts can usually provide a listing of certified mediators. Most family counselors and lawyers are also able to make referrals. Finding a mediator you feel comfortable with is similar to the search for a family therapist. The best advice is to get a referral from a trusted outside party and to ask for references that you can check. Certification requirements vary from state to state, and in many cases being certified only means that the mediator has completed a course. Make sure you ask about the mediator's level of experience with cases like yours. Lastly, if you feel the mediator is not helping to create a partnership in the resolution of your conflict, voice your concerns, and if necessary, find another mediator.

Communication Techniques That Unite

The nature of our communication during conflict has the potential to divide us even further or to unite us. In Chapter 10 we reviewed some divisive communication styles. In win-win conflict resolution it is important both to avoid those pitfalls and to choose to communicate with each other in ways that will bring us together. Active listening and assertive informing, covered in Chapters 11 and 12, are two such ways of communicating. Divisive communication highlights the differences between us. Communication techniques that unite emphasize the commonalities we share. They help to create the "we." This section discusses a few more examples of communication techniques that unite.

Creating Resonance

Sheila is on the plane going home from her mediation with her former employer. The mediation is complete, and the two parties have reached an agreement. More important, they reached an understanding of the conflict itself: how it began, what escalated it, and how it could be resolved. The two parties didn't always agree on the interpretation of events, but resonance was created. Resonance is probably the most powerful communication tool available for uniting two people who are in conflict.

Resonance was created because both Sheila and the other party were able to express their own deep feelings and concerns, and to hear each other's. They were able to hear the ring of truth in each other's words. They were able to recognize that both parties' concerns were familiar, human, universal concerns—to recognize them as something each might have felt given similar circumstances. They were able to recognize themselves in the other person. In so doing, they regained respect for each other and then expressed that respect.

Reframing

After resonance was created, the two parties were able to enter the process of discussing solutions. They were willing to take each other's needs seriously. They reframed the conflict by asking, "How can we both get our needs met?"

Recall the discussion of reframing from Chapter 1. In reframing a conflict, the focus of the dialogue shifts from being about competing *positions* to being about underlying *needs*. To reframe a conflict, each party must first be able to see their opponent as a potential partner in solving the conflict they both share. Reframing brings together your needs and your opponent's needs as joint concerns. Reframing is about turning the focus of the conflict away from the personal (what you did) and placing it on the problem (how we can resolve this). An example of a reframing statement is "How can we meet your need for _____ and my need for _____?"

In order to successfully reframe the conflict, you may first need to travel the rough road of expressing difficult feelings in order to rediscover the desire to see the other person as a partner. You may need to take steps to get ready. In Sheila's case, although before the mediation she had focused on articulating her own needs, there came a point during the mediation dialogue when the energy shifted. It was no longer just about "you" or "me." The two parties began to come together. They were ready. (More about creating readiness is discussed in the next section.)

In this case it was the mediator who recognized the readiness and reframed the discussion by suggesting that the disputants explore solutions. Sheila's personal readiness, followed by the mediator's reframing, enabled her to think about solutions that not only met her own needs, but also met the other party's needs. Likewise, the other disputant was able to move in his position and to offer proposals. Together the two reached a joint agreement.

In the above example it was the mediator who reframed. However, we don't always have the advantage of a neutral third party. Sometimes the dialogue is just between two people. Either party can reframe when both parties are beginning to come together.

Here are some examples of reframing statements that can occur within a dialogue:

Divisive statement: "All you ever want to do is watch TV. We don't go out or see any of our friends unless they come here."

Reframing statement: "You like to watch TV, and I like to go out dancing. The problem is when I'm out and you're in the house we hardly get to spend time together. How can we spend more time together, and at the same time let each of us do what we like?"

Divisive statement: "This job doesn't pay enough, man. I can't keep working like this for no money."

Reframing statement: "I really need to make more money at this job, but I understand your budget constraints. How can I increase my income without overstressing your budget?"

Creating Readiness

When the parties in a conflict lack access to a third party to help them express themselves, readiness to come together can still be initiated by one of the parties. This can occur in several ways:

Finding Commonalities

If the parties are already interacting (as in an ongoing work relationship), one of the parties can initiate conversations that bring out the commonalities they share. These can include commonalities of interest separate from the conflict between them. In fact, in looking for commonalities it's often best to look for topics unrelated to the conflict between the two parties. That way they're interacting on neutral ground, so to speak. Side talk about their common interests, preferences, opinions, and experiences can help promote good feelings between the parties and help prepare them to solve the problem.

Linda and George worked in the kitchen of a fast-food restaurant. The efficiency of the team was being questioned by management. This promoted a lot of tension among the workers. Linda and George blamed each other for slowdowns in productivity, and an interpersonal "war" developed between them. At home, talking about the situation with his wife, George decided that he wanted to ease the tension. He wanted the war with his coworker to stop. Eventually he would have to talk with her about the issues at hand—the work-related procedures—but he knew they were not yet ready for that dialogue. It would just break out into a shouting match. So he decided to ease the tension another way. He knew Linda was having difficulties finding the right child care. He asked her how it was going. He showed concern. Actually, the concern was real because he also had a young son, and finding child care had been an ongoing issue in his life.

The challenge of finding good child care was a commonality shared by Linda and George that had nothing to do with the conflict they were embroiled in. The conversations they had about the topic of child care eased the tension between them and helped form a bond. They could see each other as "we" through their discussions about this common life problem. Eventually they carried over that "we" feeling to the problem at hand. They were able to solve the problems related to procedures at work so that productivity was increased and neither of them was blamed by the other or by management.

Sharing Rituals

Another way two people in conflict can come together is to share activities or rituals. By rituals, we mean routine behaviors. For example, brushing teeth is a ritual many couples engage in every morning. An example of a ritual in the workplace might be setting up a conference room for a meeting. Two people who want to try to work out a resolution to a conflict can engage in rituals such as preparing the discussion space, getting refreshments, etc. If they share that experience, then they are sharing an experience that has the potential to help them see each other as partners in the more serious matter of problem solving.

The examples mentioned above may seem like trivial activities, but rituals such as these help set a tone. Tone makes all the difference in problem solving. Solutions can be found if both parties are willing to try to find solutions. That willingness is all-important, and promoting that willingness is the purpose of activities that create the "we."

Allowing Time to Pass

Sometimes it just takes time for two people in conflict to feel ready to see each other as partners in the process. In previous chapters we discussed the necessity sometimes of taking a break from a conflict in order to allow intense feelings to subside. Once the intense feelings subside, people often remember the positive feelings they felt for each other and reach the desire to work things out. However, we also discussed a few cautions related to allowing time to pass. These bear repeating. First, resist waiting too long to return to addressing the conflict. When you are no longer interacting with the other person and feel relatively safe from the disturbing emotions of conflict, it may be tempting to stay away, to avoid the conflict altogether. Although some situations lend themselves to that solution, it is sometimes impossible to escape permanently. It may instead be necessary to work out a solution. Second, be aware that ruminating (discussed in Chapter 2) could refuel your anger (or the other party's anger). Distance plus rumination could backfire. In that case the passing of time makes the problem worse, not better.

There are many ways to create the "we" in a conflict. Sometimes bringing in a third party to mediate the dispute is the answer. Sometimes it can be done through the ways we communicate with each other. By reframing, finding commonalities, and, when necessary, taking the time to walk away and gain perspective from a distance, we can create the peace that results from remembering that we are all in this together.

℘ Exercise: Finding the "We" in Conflict

1. Writing in your peacework journal, reframe the following divisive statements:

   "Don't touch the air conditioner. Maybe you need to move to another desk, because I can't take all that cold air."

   "Turn the TV off. All you do is watch television. We never talk about anything anymore."

   "How many times are we going to have chicken this week? I'm sick of it!"

2. Remember Marcus and Gina from Chapter 8? As you reread their scenario, what suggestions would you make that could help them find resonance? Imagine the commonalities they might have or rituals they might share as a couple.

3. Using as many of the skills from previous chapters as you like, rewrite their conversation about Gina's attire. Help them find the "we." (Hint: identify needs, use "I" mes-

sages, reframe, state commonalities, etc.) To get you started:

Marcus: "Why do you have to wear those low-cut blouses? You need to change your clothes."

Gina: "I shouldn't have said what I did about your clothes. I know you like to look good, and so do I."

(Continue from here.)

Part IV

ℒℒ

Creating Peace

CHAPTER 14

ॐ

Negotiating a Conflict

In Parts I and II, we took a close look at conflict and at what happens to us physiologically and psychologically when we're in the middle of one. In Part III, we explored the concept of creating partnership in conflict. We developed skills for establishing resonance during conflict so that we can work together to find resolution. In Part IV we will progress from learning the dance steps to getting out on the floor and dancing. We will move from preparing to create peace to an exploration of the skills and conditions that are necessary to actually carve out, with our partner, the peaceful resolution we desire.

A conflict begins when two people perceive a disagreement: when they realize that they seem to want different things, or when their differences in opinion become apparent. Most of the time we deal with our everyday conflicts successfully and automatically. However, other times further steps are necessary. At such times the parties can consciously engage each other in negotiation to resolve the conflict.

A negotiation can be simple or complex, formal or informal, spontaneous or planned. Regardless, there are phases through which the parties pass on the way to resolution. In this chapter, we will explain the phases by describing a relatively informal negotiation process two people used to resolve an interpersonal conflict.

The same phases can also apply to more formal and complex negotiations.

Phase 1: Getting Ready

Earlier chapters have delineated factors that might affect how we handle a conflict: our past history, the history of the conflict, our perceptions about what happened, our habitual responses to conflict, our immediate physical and emotional states, and more. We have recommended skills that are helpful in bringing people to the point where they are ready to work out a solution: cooling down, centering, reflecting, separating the past from the present, and returning to the present. Additionally, we have discussed communication skills that can be used to help engage the other person, to help them calm down and get ready to work out a solution. All of these tools together form part of the first stage of a negotiation: getting ready. Let's look at how a married couple used some of these tools in preparing to resolve a conflict, and let's look at a few additional tools they used to help them get ready.

Emotional Preparation:
Reflection and Self-Examination

Cleo and Sal had a conflict about their vacation plans. He wanted to go to New York City for a five-day weekend in September. She wanted to go to the Jersey Shore for two weeks in July. Every time the issue came up it would end in stalemate, with both of them walking away, grumbling.

She would dig in her heels and say, "You always get your way about these things. We've gone where you wanted to go so many times. Now it's my turn."

He would say, "That's not true! You get your way at least as much as I do!"

She would say, "All I want is a relaxing vacation with you, two whole weeks of hanging out together with nothing but the sun and nature to keep us company."

He would say, "You know I can't get away for that long with my business so new. And I'd go crazy just staring at the ocean.

What about the theater and fine restaurants like we always talked about? Don't you think you'd have fun doing that?"

She would say, "Your business always comes first!"

He would say, "It's not just my business. It's our livelihood. You know I don't like the beach anyway. You're just thinking about yourself!"

And on and on. Stuck. They were both pulling for what they wanted. They tried to convince the other of the merits of their respective positions; then, when that didn't seem to work, they attacked each other. The conflict had developed a history of escalation that made both of them stubbornly hold on to what they said they wanted.

Then there was a break in the tension. It came about as a result of a change in tactic Cleo made. During breakfast one morning she said, "Look, Sal. This vacation argument is getting us nowhere. I really would like to work it out. I want both of us to be happy with what we decide. So why don't we take some time after dinner tonight to just try to talk about it."

Sal thought about it. At first he said, "Isn't that what we've been trying to do?"

"Well, yeah. But not really. We've both just been trying to get our way. Why don't we do a little creative thinking together? Let's see what we can come up with."

Sal agreed. During the day he thought about the situation they were in—about all the bad feelings that were accumulating between them as a result of this conflict. He realized that for some reason the issue had become larger than just where to go on vacation. In some way they were making the issue a proving ground, a power struggle. Upon further reflection he could see that he was having such a strong reaction against the beach because the idea of going to the beach brought up unpleasant memories of family beach excursions that were full of arguments. He decided that he needed to just let go of all those issues and all that baggage. None of that had anything to do with what would help Cleo and him have a good time together.

Whether a conflict takes place in a personal relationship, as with Cleo and Sal, or in a workplace relationship, each party must engage in self-examination. Many workplace conflicts have characteristics that remind a person of family conflicts. Many marital conflicts reflect issues that each partner experienced in their family of origin. It's important in preparing to negotiate any conflict to "unhook" oneself from those associations—to be able to see clearly what the present-day conflict is really about.

By suggesting a time later in the day to try to think creatively, Cleo had given Sal the opportunity to reflect. She also took the opportunity to reflect and found that she had all sorts of hidden issues tied up in this vacation conflict: jealousy about Sal's attention to his business, a feeling of powerlessness in the relationship, and a desire to regain some power by getting her way. By identifying these issues she was able to let go of them—at least long enough to think clearly about what kind of vacation could meet both of their needs.

Cognitive Preparation: Planning Strategies for Resolution

Besides emotional preparation, some advanced thought and analysis of the conflict can greatly enhance the chances of a successful negotiation. Things to think about include the following aspects of the conflict:

1. *Issues.* Identify the major issues in the conflict. The issues are the major categories or questions that must be dealt with. Cleo and Sal's conflict could be broken down into several issues: *where* to go, *when* to go, and *how long* to stay on vacation. To a certain extent these issues are interrelated.

2. *Positions.* Once a party has identified what she or he feels are the issues, the next step is for each party to identify her or his position on each of the issues. This is advanced preparation that each party does alone, so each one is primarily focusing on her or his own position. However, it is also advantageous to try to identify one's best guess about the other person's position: what she or he seems to be saying about what she or he wants. Since at this point much of the analysis about the other party's position is guesswork,

it's important to be open to the possibility that you may be wrong. Once the negotiation begins you'll be better able to confirm this information. Cleo wanted to go on vacation to the Jersey Shore in July for two weeks. Sal wanted to visit New York City for a five-day weekend in September.

3. *Needs.* As we discussed in Chapter 1, behind every position is an underlying need. A position is the means by which a person feels his or her need will be met. However, it is important to recognize that the position represents *only one way* to meet the need. There may be many other ways. If the needs underlying both parties' positions can be identified, then there's a greater possibility that the ways in which both parties can get their needs met can be identified.

To discover an underlying need, ask the question "Why?" Why did Sal want to go to New York City? Because he wanted to experience the cultural life there. His need was for a stimulating cultural experience. Why did he need a stimulating cultural experience? Because he felt he needed some intellectual renewal. Why did Cleo want to go to the Jersey Shore? Because she wanted to be close to nature and to swim in the ocean. Her need was to experience the calming energy of the ocean. Her need was for some physical renewal. Underneath their stated positions, they both needed renewal. His emphasis was on the intellectual. Her emphasis was on the physical.

Sal's need to vacation in September stemmed from his need to save money. September was a slow time at work. Cleo's need to vacation in July was to take advantage of when the children would be away at camp so they would not have to arrange for additional child care. That would also save them money. Sal's need to go for five days was to avoid missing too much work (another money-related need). Cleo wanted a two-week vacation because she felt they both needed that much time to adequately relax (a renewal-related need).

The following chart outlines the issues between Sal and Cleo, each party's positions, and their underlying needs.

ISSUE	WHERE		WHEN		HOW LONG	
	Position 1	Need 1	Position 2	Need 2	Position 3	Need 3
Sal	New York City	culture = intellectual renewal	Sept.	save money during slow time at work	5 days	avoid missing work and losing money
Cleo	Jersey Shore	ocean = physical renewal	July	save money on child care while kids at camp	2 weeks	time to relax and renew

4. *Alternative suggestions.* In preparing for a negotiation, it can greatly enhance the possibility of success if each party begins to think creatively about the problem. Do this by examining alternative ways of meeting both parties' needs. For example, Sal might think, "I have the most fun on vacation when there's cultural stimulation. Cleo seems to be into nature. I wonder if there's another place we can go that has what we both need." He is getting unstuck internally. During his inner dialogue he might come up with a few alternative suggestions, or he might only come up with the question. There is no need for him to solve the problem on his own. The problem solving will happen when they get together. However, he is beginning the process of thinking creatively about alternative solutions.

5. *Bargaining chips.* Part of the process of coming up with alternative suggestions might be to think about bargaining

chips. That is, based on your estimation of what the other party needs, what can you offer him or her that might meet that need? Sal felt that Cleo needed more time with him. She seemed to be expressing that. He thought maybe if he could figure out a way to take more time off, that might satisfy her need and bring them closer to agreement. However, he did not want to jeopardize his business by staying away too long. Perhaps there was something she could do that would help him rethink the time he needed to be physically at his work site. Sal was developing ideas for bargaining chips he could offer (more time) and at the same time thinking about what he might accept from her (help in rethinking his time) that he could use.

It is important once again to realize that you are only guessing about what the other person might want or need, and about what he or she might be willing to give. During the actual negotiation you might discover something you hadn't realized before.

6. *BATNA.* Roger Fisher and William Ury, in their well-known book, *Getting to Yes*, developed the term *BATNA* as an acronym for the phrase "Best alternative to a negotiated agreement." In part, this is an acknowledgment of the fact that not all agreements can be negotiated successfully. There is an advantage to thinking in advance about what you would do if you couldn't agree. What is your best alternative if you remain in stalemate? If you realize you have a very good BATNA, then you may choose to stand your ground and hold out for what you really want. For example, if you were negotiating the price of a house as a buyer and you knew there were several other houses on the market that you liked and that were less expensive, then you could offer a low price and stick to it. You wouldn't feel much pressure to bid higher in order to get the house because you knew you could get another that was just as good.

If, on the other hand, you know you have a weak BATNA, then you might need to make more concessions in order to reach an agreement. If this was the only house available in the area where you wanted to live, and you really needed to buy a house right away, in order to get the house you might decide to offer a higher price if your low bid was not accepted. If you can assess your BATNA in advance, you might be able strengthen your BATNA, thus strengthening your bargaining position. In the house negotiation, if this was the only house available in the neighborhood and you needed to move in right away, you might be able to strengthen your BATNA by investigating rental properties; renting a house for a while would allow you to take more time finding a house to buy. You could then hold out for a lower price.

When he reflected on the situation, Sal realized that there was no good alternative to agreement. If he and Cleo remained in stalemate, the vacation was at stake. Failure to come to agreement could be permanently damaging, not only to the vacation but also to their relationship. Despite the occasional arguments, they were both committed to their relationship. They needed to work out a solution. If they worked out a solution that pleased only one of them, then the relationship would be in jeopardy. On reflecting, he redoubled his commitment to coming up with a solution that pleased them both.

Phase 2: Developing a Positive Climate

An important ingredient in a successful negotiation is to develop a positive climate in which the negotiation can be conducted. This may involve

- arranging for a physical environment conducive to productive discussions with ample time allotted;

- sharing routines or "rituals" that help establish commonalities and good feelings; and

* establishing ground rules for discussion, if necessary.

Cleo and Sal decided to wait until the evening to hold their vacation discussion. They both knew they were coming home from work early enough to allow ample time to talk. It was a Friday, so the children would not need help with homework. They could get a babysitter and go out for dinner. They figured they could relax through dinner and drinks and have a leisurely discussion. The sharing of a meal at a familiar restaurant they both loved would provide a ritual that could set a positive climate. They both had a habit of cutting each other off in the midst of heated conversation. Before they began their conversation Cleo suggested that they both try hard to listen to each other and hear everything the other person had to say. Sal agreed.

Sal and Cleo had enough trust in one another and enough knowledge of what made the other comfortable to be able to easily establish a positive climate. In hostile, escalated conflict situations it might take a third party to consciously set the stage for negotiation by providing a comfortable space, offering coffee or drinks, asking if there are any ground rules the parties would like to follow, and the like. Furthermore, it helps if both parties begin by reaffirming their desire to come to a solution that meets both of their needs.

Phase 3: Establishing Positions and Needs

Generally, a negotiation begins with one or both parties initiating a discussion about positions and needs. For both parties, the tasks of this phase are

* clarifying their opening positions;

* probing for the other person's underlying needs;

* presenting one's own underlying needs; and

* identifying the most important needs for each person.

This stage has transformational potential, both for the present conflict and for the relationship as a whole. The process of recognizing each other's underlying needs is healing for the relationship. Using the communication skills of active listening and assertive informing (discussed in Chapters 11 and 12) is very helpful in having a successful discussion about positions and needs and in gaining the mutual understanding that can heal a rift.

Sal began by saying, "Look, I know you want to go to the beach, but I'd like to have a city vacation. I would like the cultural stimulation. I get bored at the beach."

Cleo answered, "The beach bores you? I didn't realize that. We could go to the movies in the evening."

"We could stay home and go to the movies. What do you love about the beach?"

"Well, I love being in a natural setting like the ocean. I need that kind of contact with nature to recharge my batteries. Why do you love going to New York City?"

"I love the opportunity to hear live music and go to the theater. It gives me a kind of creative and intellectual stimulation I don't get at my job or in my everyday life. It's like recharging my batteries as well. And I can't stay away for two weeks like you want to—not with a new business. I can't be out of touch for so long."

"So, you're concerned about being out of touch with your business. Two weeks would be too long to be out of touch?"

"Yes."

"Well, the five days you were proposing is just not enough for me. It wouldn't even feel like a vacation. I need more time away in order to relax and come back refreshed."

"You need more time? You need to feel refreshed, both by some contact with nature and by having a length of time away. Is that what you are saying?"

"Yes. And you're saying you don't want to be away a long time because you need to be in touch with your business. Also, you want to get recharged through some cultural stimulation. Is that right?"

"Yes. That's right."

In this dialogue, both Cleo and Sal were stating their positions, asking the other person questions about their underlying needs, stating their own needs, and paraphrasing to check for understanding.

Phase 4: Reframing and Organizing Issues

In this phase the tasks for both parties are

- reframing the conflict as a joint problem to be solved and

- identifying, prioritizing, and organizing key issues.

Recall our discussions of reframing from earlier in the book. In this phase of conflict negotiation, the purpose of reframing is to carry the dialogue forward in the direction of looking for solutions. Either person can reframe the discussion. A simple formula for reframing is to say: "You need 'x' and I need 'y.' How can we get both 'x' and 'y'?" Observe how different such a statement is from either "All you think about is you, you, you and what you want," or "That's a stupid idea and it just won't work." It's different because the speaker has reframed the conflict from being about "you" versus "me" to being about "we."

Cleo reframed the discussion. She said, "So you need cultural stimulation and I need contact with nature. Is there any place we can go that offers both?"

Sal said, "Good question. Let's think about that together. We also have to think about the time issue. How can you get enough time away to feel relaxed, and at the same time I don't lose touch with my business for too long?"

"Okay. That's two questions to deal with. Also, there's the issue of when, July versus September. The kids are away at camp in July. That's why I want to go then. Why do you want to go in September?"

"It's a slow season."

"July is busy for you?"

"No, not that busy. I guess that issue isn't so important for me. July would do just as well as September if we can figure out the issue of how long. Right now I'm stuck on that. Maybe you could help me."

In that dialogue both Sal and Cleo reframed the issues. They also posed them as questions, creating brainstorming topics so that the issues were organized for further discussion. At the same time they discovered that certain issues were more important than others.

Phase 5: Exploring and Choosing Solutions

The task of this phase is to seek solutions through problem solving. Two methods of problem solving are:

- formal brainstorming between both people and

- informal, focused dialogue in which bargaining chips are explored and offered.

Brainstorming

Cleo suggested looking at the "where" issue first. They both suggested a number of places that might provide Cleo with a natural setting and also provide Sal with cultural stimulation. They decided to follow a formal brainstorming procedure for this issue. As each of them came up with an idea, Cleo wrote it down on paper. While they were generating the ideas they did not comment on the idea either positively or negatively; they just wrote it down. By following the "no comment" rule, they were able to keep the ideas flowing. If they had commented on each idea as it came up, the comments might have acted to stifle the creative juices and reduce the potential number of ideas. By letting it flow, they were able to generate quite a number of potential vacation spots that could fit the bill. A goal in formal brainstorming is to go for volume so that there are a number of alternatives to choose from. It sometimes helps to set some sort of artificial "volume" goal, e.g., filling the whole page, or keeping up the brainstorming for ten minutes, or coming up with twenty alternatives. In addition, the creative process is sometimes helped if *all* ideas are written down—even ridiculous or fanciful ones such as "win the lottery."

Once enough ideas are generated, the editing phase in formal brainstorming begins. The parties can go through each idea one by one, first eliminating the ideas that don't seem feasible (e.g., camping out in Central Park) and then discussing the pros and cons of the other ideas. They finally decided on the Berkshire Mountains in Massachusetts. They decided to rent a house by a lake and close to the theater, art, music, and dance communities that existed in the surrounding towns.

Focused Problem-Solving Dialogue

Formal brainstorming did not seem appropriate for Cleo and Sal's "how long" issue. Instead, they engaged in a focused problem-solving dialogue. What sets this kind of dialogue apart from the other types of dialogue covered in this book is its exclusive focus on solving a particular issue.

Sal said, "Look. I understand you want me to spend more time with you on vacation, but this is a really crucial time for me at work. Maybe you can think of a solution that I can't."

Cleo said, "Well, as much as I hate to say this, you know your partner can always reach you by cell phone."

"That's hardly a vacation."

"I know. But…you said you could spend five days away, right?"

"Right."

"If we left after work on a Friday, then we could have the weekend. You wouldn't be in work anyhow. Then the next five days are work days. We could spend that time away with no cell phone contact except for emergencies. Then we'd have the next weekend."

"So we'd be away for nine days?"

"Wait, I'm not done. The next five days you could be in contact by cell phone. Then we could stay another weekend. We'd have almost two and a half weeks that way."

"That's pushing it, but you are on to something. I don't really think I could stay out of the office for two whole weeks, but maybe if we make the second week a three-day vacation week with cell phone, I could be back in the office by Thursday and Friday. That would mean you would have twelve days away, not the fourteen you wanted, but still a substantial amount of time. What do you think?"

"Okay, okay. Twelve days. The last three with cell phone. What if I stayed through the end of the week alone?"

"Alone in the house by yourself?"

"Maybe Myra would want to join me. I need some time with my sister."

"That could work."

In this dialogue both Sal and Cleo offered bargaining chips. Cleo offered the ideas that Sal could use the cell phone to stay in touch with his business, and that her sister could join her for the last few days. She agreed to Sal's leaving after twelve days. Sal offered to stay a few extra days beyond the original five and acted favorably toward Cleo's idea of spending the rest of the week with her sister.

This dialogue succeeded because they each were committed to working out a solution that met both parties' needs and were open to suggestions from the other person. They heard proposals from each other and packaged ideas together to form an overall solution they both liked.

Phase 6: Closing the Negotiation

This phase involves two steps:

1. *Clarifying, specifying, and confirming agreements.* The solution is incomplete without making sure each party understands what they are both agreeing to, with all the details spelled out. Sometimes the parties are so pleased to be on the road to resolution that they ignore spelling out the details. This can give rise to misunderstandings and conflicts later. It is helpful for each party to repeat to the other what he or she is agreeing to do. Alternatively, the parties can put the agreements in writing in the form of an informal list or as a formal agreement they both sign— whichever feels most appropriate.

2. *Creating follow-up and contingency plans.* Certain aspects of an agreement might require either follow-up or contingency planning. For example, Cleo decided to stay in their rented house with her sister after Sal left. What if her sister couldn't do it? Also, they decided to rent a house in the Berkshires by a lake and close to cultural events. What if they couldn't find such a house for the time and price they needed? Both Sal and Cleo needed to discuss all these possibilities and generate a few alternative contingencies. They also needed to keep their hearts, minds, and dialogue open while making plans so they could come up with more alternatives if need be.

Negotiating a resolution that will meet both people's needs takes time, thoughtfulness, and energy. It rarely happens by accident or as a result of a shouting match. Careful and close attention must be paid to the needs of each person. Suggestions and alternatives must be given that don't turn into positions, and, finally, the commitment to meeting the needs of all involved in the conflict must be upheld.

We don't always end up in conflict with individuals who are skilled or even interested in creating peaceful resolution. In the next chapter we will explore strategies for engaging in conflict when the going is rough and the tough get tougher.

℘ Exercise: Negotiating a Real-Life Conflict

Before engaging in this exercise, take some time to reflect on the exercises you completed in Chapters 4, 10, 11, and 13. Read over your journal entries as a refresher and a reminder of the skills you want to use.

1. Identify a conflict that you currently are involved in that you want to resolve. Please do not select a very heated or difficult conflict. As a place to begin, look for a simple disagreement or minor conflict. It's important to practice the negotiation steps in a situation where the risk is low; that

way, if you have difficulty or make a mistake, you will avoid
the added stress of extreme emotion.

2. In your peacework journal, write your answers to the following questions: What is the conflict about, and who is it
with? Is there only one issue, or are there several related
issues? List each of the related conflict issues you are having with this person. (For now, let's deal only with related
issues. If there are issues unrelated to the one you want to
work on now, keep your focus on this one area. You can
begin a new negotiation once this conflict is resolved.)
What do you think you need in this situation? What do
you think the other person needs?

3. Using the information you gained from answering the
questions in step 2, complete the chart below:

ISSUE

	Position 1	Need 1	Bargain-ing chips	Position 2	Need 2	Bargain-ing chips
Your name						
Name of conflict partner						

4. Now it's time to begin to engage the other person in the
resolution process. You will need to make contact with
them. Before you do, practice the breathing and centering
exercises in Chapter 3. Even if you do not feel a great deal
of stress, these are good practices to make a habit of before
any negotiation. When you contact the other person,
explain that you want to resolve the disagreement and,
with their input, select a time and a place to do so. Remember the conditions of a positive climate as you make your
arrangements. (If the climate is positive during your initial

discussion with the other person, and if it is convenient for each of you, the negotiation can begin immediately.)

5. If there is a break between contacting your conflict partner and beginning the negotiation, complete the breathing and centering exercises again just before you meet for negotiation. Open up the negotiation by stating the issues in the conflict as clearly as you can. Reemphasize your desire to work out the conflict together.

6. Probe for your partner's position and needs. Make sure you use your active listening skills to ensure understanding. Present your underlying needs, and allow your partner to ask questions or probe. Summarize the needs you heard were most important to each of you. Make sure your partner agrees that you have captured his or her most important needs in the conflict.

7. Reframe the conflict as a problem that you both need to solve. Try to use your skills in reframing—eliminate any divisive expression. If you find that you have made a divisive statement, back up and reframe. It's okay if you make a mistake. Once you become aware of it, work to correct it.

8. Identify all of the related issues and prioritize them. Remember, you are a team in this effort, so don't do all of the talking. Let your partner have a say regarding the relative importance of each of the issues.

9. Determine possible solutions by brainstorming or problem solving. Deciding when to formally brainstorm and when to use your bargaining chips and engage in focused problem solving is most frequently a judgment call. If you feel you have bargaining chips that can help in finding solutions to the issues you face, then focused problem solving is the suggested route to take. Where you have few or no bargaining chips, brainstorming is an excellent process.

10. Clarify your agreements, making sure that you both thoroughly understand what you have agreed to. Ask your part-

ner to state the solutions you have both agreed to. If you think anything has been left out or incorrectly stated, clarify by describing what you believed the agreement to have been. Remember to state where you have agreement as well as where you have differences in interpretation. If you need to revisit step 9 to come to an acceptable solution, do so at this point. If you are both ready to accept the agreement as stated, move on to the next step.

11. Develop a contingency plan in case one or more parts of the solution cannot be implemented. Also, make sure you have a mechanism for checking in with one another to ensure that the agreement is working for you both. This can be as simple as deciding you will call one another in a specified amount of time or at certain points in the process of the agreement.

12. Reflect on the negotiation. In your peacework journal write down your thoughts and feelings about the negotiation process. How did it go? Was it difficult, or was it easier than you thought it might be? What do you think you did particularly well during the negotiation? How might you do things differently the next time? What did you learn about your conflict-solving partner during this negotiation?

CHAPTER 15

℘℈

Dealing with Difficult People

Gayle remembers the following experience from her first job out of college:

> When I reentered the world of work after graduating from college, I embarked upon what I thought was a journey into a new world. I believed that the realm of work I had left behind, involving manual labor and minimum wage, was being replaced by one built around respect and learning.
>
> About five months into my new life as a management trainee for a Wall Street clearinghouse bank, I had an extraordinary experience that shaped much of my professional behavior for many years. One morning I arrived at my desk an hour early, as I usually did, and took time to savor my first sip of coffee. In a moment I would get to the reports I was responsible for monitoring (and working hard to understand). But just for that moment I wanted to unwind from the rush of the subway and gain a little distance from the whirlwind of activity that would soon mark the start of another Wall Street day.
>
> I was startled when the door opened. Traders rarely came to the operations side of the office floor, and certainly not so early in the morning. The most junior trader walked in. Smiling, he said, "Ian wants to see you." I replied, "I'll come over in a couple of minutes."

I knew that Ian, the head FX trader, wanted to speak with me about an action I'd taken the night before. After everyone on the trading floor had gone home, along with my managers and most of my colleagues, two of the best processors in the department came to me with a problem involving a trading contract. Based upon their description, the contract contained a huge error, though I admit I did not fully understand their explanation of the error. These were the two most senior processors, with years of experience, and I trusted their judgment. They advised me to have the contract backed out of the system, an action only I could authorize, and I took their advice. When Ian asked to see me, I knew that he wanted to discuss something involving that contract, and I immediately felt uncomfortable.

Less than five minutes later, the junior trader was back again. "If I were you, I'd get in there now," he said. I turned to him, with an authority I did not feel, and said, "My day is scheduled to start at 8:30, it's 7:35, I'll be on the trading floor in a couple of minutes." Turning away, I began to feel the kind of panic I sometimes experienced just before an exam.

My mind began reeling with thoughts and emotions. I took a few deep breaths, looked out the expansive office windows, and calmed my mind. I decided I had done my best. Not fully understanding the problem, I had taken wise counsel, and if there was an issue, I would be honest and would take responsibility. In those few moments, I began to regain my center.

At 7:45 I willed my legs to move and walked onto the FX trading floor. Within seconds I was blasted by a loud and demanding Ian. "Who the h—— gave you the authority to touch my ticket? You don't…" At that moment something in me shifted. I was willing to take responsibility, and unwilling to feel powerless. I stopped listening to him, took a deep breath and said, "I'm sorry, it's very early and I can't hear you when you speak that loudly. If you could explain to me what the problem is, I will do my best to straighten it out."

Everyone near us was quiet. Ian looked me in the eyes for a moment and said, in a conversational tone, "Why was my ticket cancelled? There is no reason why you or anyone else should cancel my tickets." I informed him of the problem I had been presented with the night before. I explained that I had been advised to cancel the trade by experienced staff, and I assured him that I would look into the matter and make sure it was straightened out. In the meantime the ticket would be reentered into the trading system.

As it turned out, I had been set up by the senior processors who advised me to reverse the trade. Angry that neither of them had been chosen for the management position, and insulted by the idea of working for someone younger than they were, they decided to undermine me. They knew I would get a real tongue-lashing and possibly would lose a good deal of credibility by canceling the trade ticket. Ian was considered a difficult person by the trading and support staff. He was not only the most powerful person on the FX trading desk, but he enjoyed intimidating others. It was assumed that I would leave the trading floor humiliated. But what happened was just the opposite, and it was all due to my maintaining my center (my internal power), staying focused and in the present, communicating without attacking, and being willing to take responsibility for what might have gone wrong.

What Gayle managed to accomplish during those challenging few minutes is what this chapter is about: how to maintain your center and stay focused on your goal of assertive conflict resolution even when dealing with difficult people.

Who Are These Difficult People?

First, it bears pointing out that the term *difficult person* can promote divisiveness, the very mindset we warn against throughout this book. After all, even the most difficult person would probably be offended if you called them that to their face, and doing so certainly would hinder the cause of creating a win-win resolution with that individual. It's also worth acknowledging that many people whom we perceive as difficult probably aren't difficult under all circumstances. A coworker who everyone agrees is domineering and controlling may enjoy a cooperative enough relationship with her or his spouse. Maybe she's difficult because her high-stress work environment brings that out in her. Or maybe he's difficult because he knows no other way to function as a boss. Or maybe she's having a really bad year and is coping by striking out at everyone around her. Furthermore, a lot of what makes a person seem difficult to me or to you may be about that mysterious thing called chemistry that exists between individuals. In other words, difficulty is often in the eye of the beholder.

On the other hand, some people seem hard to get along with no matter the circumstances or personalities they come in contact with. And still others are downright abusive, to the point of endangering people who try to get close to them. *Let us emphasize that if you think you're in an abusive situation, it is imperative to take action to protect yourself.* One way to start is by reading the section that appears later in this chapter, titled "When Is It Difficult, When Is It Abuse?"

The point of this chapter is not to arm you with a checklist so that you can run around identifying people as "difficult" or "not difficult." Indeed, recognize the risks against peaceful conflict resolution inherent in labeling anyone "difficult." Doing so can encourage the "me" versus "you" mindset this whole book seeks to sidestep. Still, if for whatever combination of reasons you experience someone as difficult—even if everyone else in the world insists that person is Mr. or Ms. Congeniality—then this chapter can provide you with some insights and strategies for dealing assertively with him or her. At the same time, use the processes provided elsewhere in the book to continue to reflect on the reasons *why* this particular person pushes your buttons. Is he or she triggering deeper issues that might have a lot to do with your personal history, your cultural background, or your history with this person? These are valuable questions to ponder, even while you learn the skills for dealing with difficult people.

We use the term *difficult people* to mean people who tend to embrace win-lose conflict styles. They believe that only one party in a conflict can have their needs met (or even considered). They use strategies that create or strengthen the appearance of an imbalance of power, especially when the other party is flustered or off center. Difficult people come in all shapes, sizes, and colors. There is no culture, race, or family that has a monopoly on difficult people. They can exhibit very different behaviors from one another. But the overarching characteristics of people who fall into this category are an unwillingness or an inability to consider another person's needs or feelings, and an all-consuming focus on having things their own way.

As has been discussed throughout this book, resolving a conflict successfully requires that we be aware of our own needs and the needs of others. Difficult people focus only on their own needs and then use strategies that have worked for them over and over again to win their way through a disagreement. Ian, the manager of the FX trading desk at Gayle's former place of employment, frequently used the power of his position to escalate conflict and intimidate staff. Over the years, Gayle saw him use those strategies "successfully" many times. Of course, their real success is doubtful, because people were left feeling powerless to get their needs met. And, not surprisingly, his trading staff had an unusually high turnover rate.

Strategies of Difficult People

The strategies employed by people whom others experience as difficult are ones that strengthen their position in an argument or conflict. If you think of the times when you have felt there was nothing you could do in a conflict except give in to the other person, you could probably write a list similar to the one below. The following are some strategies used by difficult people:

Deflecting Attention

Difficult people may use crying, tantrums, or other deflective strategies. They may shift into such tactics very early in a conflict, often surprising the other party, to shift attention away from the problem that needs to be solved. The behavior results in the other party concentrating on making the behavior stop, instead of on getting their own needs met. (It is important to note that crying is not always a deflective strategy. A person may be genuinely sad, upset, or angry in a conflict, and as a result begin to cry. However, when these behaviors are exhibited in the very early stages of a conflict, or if the behavior appears to be out of sync with the level of intensity of the conflict, there's a good chance that deflective strategies are being deployed.)

Consider the following dialogue between two roommates:

Sharon: Cynthia, we need to talk about the mess in the apartment.

Cynthia: What do you mean?

Sharon: Look around. Don't you think we need to do something to clean this place up?

Cynthia (eyes begin to tear up, voice chokes): Every roommate I've ever had said I was a slob. I hope you're not going to start complaining too. (Openly crying now.) I don't want to lose another roommate, and I'm just really busy at work. Oh God.

Sharon: Look, it's okay. I didn't mean to upset you. I'll just straighten things up around here this week.

Intimidation

Intimidation can be delivered loudly, in a conversational tone, or whispered. It can also be nonverbal, accomplished with long stares or menacing gestures. In the workplace, intimidation often comes from the difficult person's level of authority in the organization. Physical size can also be used to intimidate. It is the difference in power or influence that weighs heavily here.

Intimidation takes the focus off of the problem and causes the conflicted person to focus on his or her own potential discomfort. The overarching consideration becomes, how can I avoid displeasing the difficult person? The wish to appease replaces the original need in the conflict. (Note: In this case the individual who feels intimidated is *not* concerned about their safety, which would signal abuse.)

Sharon: Cynthia, we need to talk about the mess in the apartment.

Cynthia (standing up and moving closer to Sharon, without breaking eye contact): What?

Sharon (less confidently): I think we need to talk about the way the apartment looks.

Cynthia: Look, this is *my* apartment. I don't appreciate your coming in here and telling me you think it's messy. You pay rent for your bedroom and the bathroom. The living room and kitchen are available to you, but you don't decide whether they look acceptable or not. If that doesn't work for you, then maybe this arrangement won't work out. (Muttering) I don't have to take this crap.

Sharon walks away.

Ambushing

This strategy takes the form of a surprise attack, often unrelated to the current conflict. The difficult person will draw on some knowledge of the other party, or of their relationship, and use it to place them at a disadvantage, or to throw them off their center.

Sharon: Cynthia, we need to talk about the mess in the apartment.

Cynthia: And while we're at it, today is the thirty-first. I assume I'm going to get the rent on time this month. Last month you didn't pay me until the third. There is no way I can get my check to the mortgage company by the fifth if you don't give me your check by the first of every month. That *is* what we agreed to, isn't it?

Sharon: Yes it is.

Cynthia: Okay, good. For a minute I thought I was crazy and hadn't made that clear. I'm glad that's straightened out.

Sharon: Do you think we can make some arrangement to keep the common rooms straight?

Cynthia: Well, we'll see. But I don't have time to talk about that right now, I was just going to grab my coat when you came in. Maybe later. (Cynthia leaves.)

Escalation

Each of the strategies identified thus far can potentially escalate a conflict. The resulting frustration of the party attempting to deal with the issue can cause the conflict to explode. However, here we are specifically exploring the strategy of using escalating language, behavior, and tone of voice to rapidly create discomfort. Yelling, cursing, and ignoring up the ante in a conflict. They usually call for a fight. If the other party is unprepared for a fight, the difficult person can potentially cause them to back down and let go (temporarily) of the conflicting issue.

It may be surprising to see *ignoring* identified here as an escalating behavior. If you think back, however, to a time when you attempted to deal with a problem you had with someone and they refused to give you their attention, you may remember experiencing an increased level of anger. Escalation is similar to intimidation in its result, but here the emphasis is on the communication process rather than on the difference in power or influence that exists between the parties.

> *Sharon*: Cynthia, we need to talk about the mess in the apartment.
>
> *Cynthia*: (Sighs and continues to read the paper.)
>
> *Sharon*: Cynthia, did you hear what I said?
>
> *Cynthia* (to herself): I wonder if they found that little boy who was lost over on Cleveland Avenue yesterday? (Turns a page of the newspaper.)
>
> *Sharon*: So, you're just going to ignore me? Fine. Clean up the mess yourself! (Sharon storms out of the room.)

Between peers, all of the strategies listed above tend to "work" only for a while. However, if there is a power imbalance in the relationship, such as between parent/child, teacher/student, or boss/ employee, the more powerful party may be able to shut down all attempts to deal fairly with the issue. In either case, these strategies fail to provide a process for dealing with the needs of both the parties involved. They close rather than open communication, place continued focus on winning versus losing, and keep the parties feeling distant from each other, rather than creating the sense of "we" that is an important part of successful and assertive conflict resolution.

How to Deal with a Difficult Person

The reason we label some people "difficult" is precisely because we find it hard to deal with them. Employing all of the strategies we've discussed throughout this book will help, starting with breathing deeply, centering yourself, staying present to your thoughts and feelings, reframing the situation to include the needs of both parties, and using "I" messages and active listening to keep the charge out of the communication.

It will take more time to create the "we" when in conflict with a difficult person. Acknowledging the other party's needs and expressing a willingness to work toward meeting those needs is critical in any conflict, but especially those involving a difficult person. Additionally, remember to express your own needs, and to stay focused on the problem. If you continue to focus on the problem and the underlying needs, the difficult person is unable to hijack the situation. Eventually (though not necessarily the first time it is raised), the problem will be dealt with—either because one of the parties leaves the relationship, or through dialogue.

Let's look again at a conversation between roommates Sharon and Cynthia. Notice this time how Sharon manages to stay focused on her initial concern, getting the apartment cleaned up:

> *Sharon*: Cynthia, we need to talk about the mess in this apartment.
>
> *Cynthia*: And while we're at it, today is the thirty-first. I assume I'm going to get the rent on time this month. Last month you didn't pay me until the third. There is no way I can get my check to the mortgage company by the fifth if you don't give me your check by the first of every month. That *is* what we agreed to, isn't it?

Sharon: Yes, it is. So we have two things we need to talk about. I'd like to deal with the way the apartment looks in the areas we share.

Cynthia: Well, I need my money.

Sharon: I had planned to write you a check tomorrow when I get my automatic deposit. But I can write it tonight if you wait until the morning to deposit it.

Cynthia: Okay, that will work.

Sharon: Good. So let's talk about setting up some kind of cleaning schedule, or guidelines for how we keep things straight in the common areas. I have some ideas.

Cynthia: I don't really have time to get into all that now.

Sharon: Okay, but I don't want it to just drop. I can understand how getting your rent on time is important to you; and to me, having a nice environment is important. So I want to make sure we talk about it. When is a good time for you?

Cynthia: Well, really, I'm not meeting my friends for another hour. I guess we can do it now—for about fifteen or twenty minutes.

In this case, Sharon doesn't back down when Cynthia employs the ambushing strategy. Instead, she works successfully to meet Cynthia's need (to be paid rent on time). Though it takes several attempts by Sharon, Cynthia is eventually ready to deal with the problem of the disorderly apartment. However, she might have continued to exhibit difficult behavior and used several different strategies throughout the conflict. She might have moved from ambushing to escalation to intimidation to deflection.

The process of coming to resolution in a conflict with someone who uses these strategies is often very lengthy. The key in such a situation is to remain focused on the problem, as well as on the needs that surface. As you employ your resolution strategies, you may become frustrated because the behaviors and strategies of the other person do not change. Don't let the difficult person derail your desire to confront the problem. Continue to communicate in ways that honor both your own needs and the needs of the other party, and that create opportunities to bring resolution for you both.

Using the skills identified in this book does not guarantee an easy resolution, or any resolution at all. Because difficult people tend to focus only on their own needs and see conflict as a win-lose contest, they may choose not to partner with you in finding a mutually satisfying resolution.

When Is It Difficult, When Is It Abuse?

Although the difficult person is focused solely on winning the argument or getting their way, their intention is not to injure or control the other party over time. Difficult people have a fixed view of conflict that allows them to operate only from a win-lose paradigm, at least under certain circumstances. This does not make them abusers.

Abuse is defined by *Webster's* as "improper treatment; to do wrong to; to injure, dishonor, or violate." And yet, a person's actions may injure another but not necessarily be considered abusive. For example, Gayle may shout out her daughter's name to call her for dinner, thinking her daughter is in another room. Gayle is unaware that her daughter has walked up behind her, about to ask her a question. The daughter is frightened by Gayle's outburst and begins to cry. Clearly Gayle has injured her, but it wasn't abuse.

What's needed is a look at *why* the behavior occurs. Is it *intended* to injure? In her book *Ditch That Jerk*, Pamela Jayne writes:

> Controlling and abusive behavior, physical or emotional, is intentional. [It is designed] to
>
> ❂ Humiliate or embarrass you
>
> ❂ Isolate you from other people and increase your dependence on the abuser
>
> ❂ Make you feel rotten about yourself

- Scare you so you don't get out of line

- Make the point that the abuser is in control

- Get you to blame yourself for the abuser's behavior.

In Gayle's experience working in the field of conflict resolution, abusers create environments that are unsafe for their targets. These may be home or work environments, though the majority of the research to date has focused on domestic abuse. The abuse may take verbal, emotional, or physical forms, and all are harmful. The target of the abuse exists in an environment of fear, marked by dominance and subjugation. According to the book *When Men Batter Women*, by Neil Jacobson and John Gottman, who studied physical violence in couples, this is the very purpose of abuse.

The result of living with verbal abuse is severe damage to the inner well-being of the target. According to Patricia Evans in *The Verbally Abusive Relationship*, the following is a list of observed consequences of verbal abuse:

- Distrust by the individual of their own spontaneity

- Loss of enthusiasm

- Being in an on-guard state

- Concern that something is wrong with oneself

- Loss of self-confidence

- Increase in self-doubt

- Internalizing the "critical voice"

- Anxiety and fear of being crazy

- Wanting to run away or escape

- Reluctance to come to conclusions [or make decisions]

- Living in the future: "Everything will be great when/after...."

- Distrust of future relationships

(Brackets signify authors' addition.)

Whether the abuse is verbal, physical, or a combination of both, the result is an emotional toll that no one should have to suffer. Much has been written on the subject of abuse, and there is conflicting information regarding its causes, the stages of escala- tion, and what conditions create change in the abuser's behavior. It is important to state clearly that the techniques for conflict resolution and creating peace that are described in this book *will not change the behavior of an abuser*. Abusers do not care about their target or their relationship to the target, except to the extent that they maintain control.

If you suspect—and we mean if you have the slightest inkling—that you are in an abusive relationship, seek outside help. Contact a therapist, family counselor, victim hotline (where you will be provided with resources for help), or local law enforcement agency (in the case of physical abuse). But, first and foremost, make plans for your safety and well-being. This often means leav- ing the relationship. In *When Men Batter Women* Jacobson and Gottman write, "Sadly, all of the factors that led to decreases in violence were characteristics of the batterers themselves. In other words, there was nothing [the target] could do to stop the abuse except *get out of the relationship*." (Emphasis added.)

Leaving is often a difficult decision for those who are abused. But it is a necessary one. We have encountered several women, in our professional and personal lives, who believed that if they could just change themselves in some fundamental way, their relation- ships would get better. The findings of Jacobson and Gottman make it clear that changes in the target's behavior or thinking fail to decrease violence. Taking responsibility for every nuance in a relationship in an attempt to create peace is a no-win solution. This is because abusers are not interested in peace; they are only concerned with domination.

As Pamela Jayne points out in *Ditch That Jerk*, the payoff for the abuser of their behavior is a sense of power, winning, being right all of the time, making all of the decisions in the relation- ship, and getting others to do things for them. The fundamental principles of peaceful conflict resolution are in direct contradic- tion to this paradigm of behavior and thought. The principles of peaceful conflict resolution call for being inclusive and open, practices that can place the peacemaker in the vulnerable position of revealing their feelings and needs. The abuser can then use this heightened vulnerability to his or her advantage.

When faced with an abusive situation, the target's first responsibility is for his or her own safety. Remove yourself and get support. Do not attempt to create peace by hanging in there and taking the punishment being offered. If you must continue to work through a conflict with an abusive person, the next chapter will explore what you can do when the other person is intent on making war.

CHAPTER 16

⁀℘⅏

Interpersonal War and Peace

The intention to create peace on the part of both parties is all-important in the effort to create peace. Both people need to share that intention before any peace effort can be successful. This chapter deals with how to handle situations in which one of the parties in the conflict has intentions *other than* creating peace.

The Intention to Escape

If one person wants to work out a conflict with another, and the other person continually and consciously intends to avoid working it out, then the conflict will not be worked out.

Louis and Sally had a fight. Louis reacted by breaking up with Sally. Sally, who was very much in love with Louis, tried to approach him again and again with an appeal to work out their differences. Louis, who was also in love with Sally, had a history of problems with commitment in relationships. His conflict with Sally fueled his fear of commitment. He refused to talk with Sally about the problem. He refused to show any willingness to work it out. Instead, he created a shield against their relationship. He got involved with another woman. No matter how Sally tried to ask Louis to work on their conflict, there was another, stronger force (his fear of commitment) that kept him in escape mode. The more Sally pursued him, the faster he ran away.

Rosa and Hope are sisters. Rosa and Hope had a conflict over the sharing of babysitting for their children. The conflict was reminiscent of fights they'd had growing up—fights over sharing responsibilities. The conflict brought up suppressed feelings of inadequacies on Hope's part, because as a child she was ridiculed by their mother and unfavorably compared to Rosa. Rosa wanted to work out their differences about sharing babysitting. She did not see it as a big problem. However, for Hope the issues were major, and she refused to discuss it. This created a further rift. Rosa resented Hope's avoidance of the issue. Hope, sensing Rosa's resentment, retreated even further. Pretty soon the two were not speaking to each other at all. Rosa appealed to Hope on a few occasions to try to solve the conflict, but Hope did not respond. The more Rosa approached her, the faster Hope tried to run away. Rosa eventually gave up, feeling she could do nothing about it.

What to Do in the Face of Another's Escape Route

Do what you can to appeal to the other to work it out, but know that what you by yourself can do is limited. Sometimes the best you can do is to let go. This can be hard, especially when it means the loss of an important relationship, but if another person refuses to engage you, there might be few other solutions. You can offer the other person concessions, apologize for what you have done wrong, and invite the other to work it out. Sometimes the passage of time will create the conditions to heal the relationship. Sometimes it won't. If those alternatives fail to work, then it might be out of your power to affect the situation. In such a case, even though it's small consolation, you can feel good about the fact that you did your best to hang in there and try to work through the problem assertively.

The Intention to Create War

If one party wants peace and, for whatever reason, the other party wants war, then you have war. Difficult emotions such as fear, hate, envy, and jealousy fuel the fires of attack and retaliation and contribute to the choice to wage interpersonal war with another. These unchecked emotions can lead to war when they are accompanied by two other elements: an outlook that justifies attack as a valuable method to get what one wants, and a belief that one can win a war (perceived power).

A person might initiate an attack because

- he/she wants something another person has (envy) and feels that he/she has the power to win a battle (perceived power)

- he/she is convinced that the other is less deserving (a form of hate)

- he/she feels that the other is less entitled (jealousy)

- he/she feels that the other is a threat (fear)

Attacks are also initiated when one party feels that the other has harmed him or her in some way, and attack is perceived as the best method for righting the wrong. The students who perpetrated the massacre of other students and adults at Columbine High School, in Colorado, were retaliating for being picked on. The repeated injury to their self-esteem was combined with a thorough acquaintance with and access to guns. The gun culture carries with it an implied approval of violence as a method of problem solving. Although many of our interpersonal wars do not involve weapons of physical violence, words can be weapons as well. And whereas most people do not resort to mass killing to correct a wrong, the combination of injury, access to weapons (verbal or otherwise), and the belief that attack is justified can result in repeated attacks on others, both verbal and nonverbal.

War can escalate out of control when either party engages in a physical or psychological "arms race." Nations have used this tactic as a method of "keeping the peace." The belief is that the enemy will realize that he or she is less powerful and will therefore refrain from attack. This method often backfires. With nations, it creates an actual buildup of weapons of destruction and the possibility that these can be used at any time. In interpersonal relationships, it creates a psychological "dare," a feeling that one cannot back down in the face of threats. It promotes an effort to build up one's own threat. For example, a young person holding a grudge against another might gather together his or her own friends to challenge the other. There may be no intention at that point of actually fighting. The belief might be that the other party will back down in the face of this show of strength. However, the act alone may escalate the conflict. The challenged person might gather together his or her own cousins, siblings, and friends. Pretty soon you have group against group—the makings of gang warfare, tinder primed for a stray spark to ignite it.

Psychological weapons can also be accumulated in an interpersonal arms race. One party can repeatedly verbally attack the other in public and private, use demonstrable means that threaten to undermine the other person's welfare, interfere with the other's well-being financially or socially, or attempt to rally outside parties to his or her side. Such a campaign initiated by one person can promote the same actions in the other. As each side seeks to threaten and damage the other, war escalates out of control. Once war gets started, attack is often met with counterattack, fueling the fire even more.

Some wars escalate so far that they become intractable. Some conflicts, such as the one in the Middle East, have such a long history of attack and counterattack that the conflict seems to have its own life. Likewise, with interpersonal conflicts, grudge wars can develop that permanently damage relationships between people.

Christine and Lara sold real estate for the same agency. The salespeople at this agency had a system worked out to prevent conflicts among the agents. They took turns approaching a potential client who walked through the door. Christine felt that Lara had violated this agreement while Christine was out getting coffee for the group. She felt that a client who was "hers" had been "stolen" from her by Lara. She retaliated by calling one of Lara's clients and showing her a house without telling Lara. This initiated a war of retaliation between them.

They each refused to show the other the support generally shared by the salespeople at their agency. Whenever they were in the same room they engaged in some form of yelling and screaming. Lara threatened to run Christine out of business by stealing her clients. In addition, Lara tried to turn others in the agency against Christine, isolating Christine from any team support. The bad feelings between them grew over time and eventually spread to the others in the agency. Other agents started taking sides—friends of Christine versus friends of Lara. By this time there were so many bad feelings between Christine and Lara that the possibility of healing the relationship was seriously diminished. The conflict made both of them unhappy since the negativity it generated entered their thoughts while they were away from work. Neither person wanted to leave the agency since it was a lucrative job in a very well positioned real estate market. They felt stuck in war.

Early on, Christine had made overtures of peace to Lara. She tried to convey through others that she wanted the war to end and she wanted to work something out. However, Lara was convinced that her anger at Christine was justified, that attack was the best and most effective method for getting what she wanted, and that she had the capacity to win this war. She believed she could make life so miserable for Christine that Christine would leave the agency. She had succeeded in doing so with others in the past.

Once her peace overtures were refused, Christine dug in her heels. She felt that she could not back down in the face of Lara's "campaign of terror." Despite the fact that friends were telling Christine to just leave the agency and find another job, Christine did not want to leave defeated. She stayed, but she felt stuck. War was escalating, and she did not know how to get out of it.

Both women had appealed to management about the conflict. Their approach had been to try to rally support for their own side by blaming the other for the war. The manager's intervention embraced the same attitude of "finding blame." He heard both stories and alternately accused one or the other woman of being wrong. It was an ineffective intervention that just made matters worse. Since both Christine and Lara were excellent salespeople, business did not suffer as a result of the war, so management failed to see any reason for further intervention.

What to Do in the Face of War

Here are some tactics you can deploy to deal assertively with the threat of interpersonal war while maintaining your goal of peace.

1. Protect yourself.

If someone is attacking you, the first and most important thing is to get out of harm's way. Protect yourself as best you can. If he or she is throwing a punch at you, then block it to the best of your ability. Duck and cover.

This may seem obvious in the case of physical harm, but less obvious when it comes to psychological violence. If you believe that someone is intending you harm and you believe they are pointing a psychological gun to your head, then protect yourself.

Psychological or verbal abuse is often aimed at the ego of the target. Recognize this. Surround yourself with people and situations that can potentially counter the damage the attacker will do. Draw on your internal resources to the best of your ability so that you can stay true to yourself and remain your own best defender. Your aim here is to avoid joining the attacker and turning against yourself. Meditate and visualize that you are surrounded by the goodness and love of the universe, and that the universe is creating a protective shield around you that keeps you safe from attacks on your psychological well-being.

If the attacker is doing actual damage to your property or financial status, then shore up the security of your financial resources. In the above example, Christine was concerned that Lara was undermining her business by stealing her clients. She needed to stay vigilant to make sure she got what she was due.

This was a strain for Christine, since under circumstances of inter-personal peace the salespeople helped each other out and did not have to worry about others stealing their business. But once war broke out, Christine lost that sense of trust and had to compensate by redoubling her vigilance. It was a strain, but she saw it as necessary.

If the attacker is violating your legal or contractual rights, then get an attorney to help protect your legal rights. Attorneys are partisan, and they specialize in protection when the law is being broken or when a dispute has escalated into a matter for the civil courts. If you hire a lawyer, she or he is on your side. Sometimes you need this assistance.

2. Use whatever nonviolent tools you can muster to defend yourself.

In the case of physical threats, do not take the law into your own hands by getting a weapon and shooting back. Do not threaten to beat up the other person. Do not throw a punch. When violence is threatened, protect yourself from aggression, but do not attack back. Violence begets more violence. Meeting violence with additional violence creates an out-of-control escalatory spiral in which both parties can get seriously hurt.

There is a street myth that if someone hits you, you must hit back to show them they can't push you around. It's a myth because the reality is that once fists are flying they don't stop. In today's gun culture, fists can easily be followed by guns, and guns kill. Stay fixed in your own intention to create peace even if you cannot see how to do it at the moment. Know that more violence is not the way.

In the midst of violence, both physical and psychological, people often "lose it." That is, they become emotionally hijacked and violent reactions take over. Cool yourself down as much as you can. Make use of the techniques for cooling down and centering that are offered earlier in this book (Chapter 3). If you find yourself becoming emotionally hijacked, then forgive yourself. Understand that it's a human response, but avoid harming the other and yourself as much as you can.

3. Improve your BATNA.

In situations of interpersonal war, Fisher and Ury's concept of BATNA ("best alternative to a negotiated agreement"; see Chapter 14) becomes very relevant. If you feel you are in the midst of a conflict that has escalated to the point that negotiation is no longer possible from your perspective, then actively generate ideas for what else you can do. In Christine's case, the conflict with Lara created a shift in her thinking about where she should be working. At first she wanted to stay right where she was. Then she began to come to terms with the fact that she felt at a loss regarding what to do about a very unpleasant situation that was adversely affecting her whole life. She began to realize that this kind of conflict was not unusual for the job she had. The job involved intense competition among coworkers in the same office. It tended to attract people who by nature were aggressive or sometimes downright ruthless. Although Christine felt she couldn't just leave her job abruptly without another alternative, she began to investigate other ways to make a living. She began to reframe the situation to herself. Instead of feeling that she needed to stay put so she wouldn't be backing down and losing, she began to feel that she needed to find an environment that was more conducive to both economic success and interpersonal peace with one's coworkers.

4. Equalize the power.

Christine felt hopeless because she thought she wanted to end the war, but the verbal and psychological violence from Lara persisted. Christine didn't know how to turn the situation around, so she began to investigate other venues for employment. Lara got her power from her persistent personality. One coworker expressed it this way: "Lara is like a pit bull when it comes to relationships." The management intervention was both ineffective and nonexistent. Equalizing the power in this situation was not an option for Christine because she did not want to summon her own "pit bull" tendencies. She felt doing so would be harmful to her sense of self in the long run.

However, there are situations in which equalizing the power is quite relevant and appropriate. Sometimes parties need motivation to change their tactics from aggressive to conciliatory, and the more they feel they have power and control in a situation, the less motivation they have to change. For example, a worker who is being harassed by a supervisor in a unionized plant may have recourse to the machinery of grievance, contract, and collective bargaining. These are hard-won gains for workers that allow them to avoid being victim to less than benevolent managerial methods. However, even in nonunion employee situations, employees have rights. They can use both legal and internal or organizational routes to defend their rights. Such rights exist to equalize power.

Another example of equalizing power is to intervene when the aggressor is trying to muster popular opinion to his or her side. If popular opinion can be used as a source of power—that is, if peer pressure can wield power in a situation by harming a target and creating a sense of social isolation in him or her—then the target can equalize power by countering such efforts. This can be accomplished by encouraging bystanders to remain neutral. Notice that we are not recommending trying to get those others on your side. Doing so can create a polarization that may eventually backfire. If people can be primed to take one side, than they can just as easily be swayed to cross over to the opposing side. The best role for bystanders is to remain neutral and to speak out to both parties in favor of creating peace.

5. Consider making a peace offering.
By *peace offering* we mean an offer that the other party finds very appealing and that will help create peace. There may come a time when a peace offering is appropriate and apparent. If you can perceive that the other party really needs something from you that you feel you can give without losing face, then offer it. For example, Sheila knows that apologies are very important to her grown daughter. When Sheila's daughter feels she has been wronged, it's very important to her that the other party apologize. Those who know Sheila's daughter know that for her an apology is a significant peace offering. However, people differ in this respect. For Sheila, apologies are nice, but she does not give them as much cre-

dence as her daughter does. So saying "I'm sorry" to Sheila would
not go as far as it would with her daughter.

In complex, intense conflict a simple apology might not work.
It might be more relevant to find a peace offering you can make
that the other party really wants. None of this was relevant for
Christina since she did not really know what Lara wanted. She had
apologized for calling Lara's customer and indicated through others that she wanted peace, but Lara seemed like she was geared for
war. The war had taken on a life of its own.

However, with a different personality type Christine might
have been able to make some headway with a peace offering.
Since Christine now felt remorse over calling Lara's client, maybe
she could have offered Lara financial compensation for loss of that
sale. Perhaps that would have calmed things down enough so that
the two could have worked out some solution.

6. Seek the intervention of a peacemaker.
Sometimes when two people cannot find their way to creating
peace by themselves, a third party can help. However, it's important to recognize that in certain cases the involvement of a third
party can inflame things. In an upsetting interpersonal war it is
very common for each party to talk to friends and potential supporters in order to rally an army of bystanders. These bystanders
do not play the role of peacemakers. In fact, they frequently make
the situation worse by cheering each party on to greater acts of
aggression.

Christine and Lara each sought the intervention of management, but the manager did not act like a peacemaker. He made
the situation worse by carrying stories each person told him to the
other. The dialogue would go like this:

Manager: Lara says you're constantly interfering with her.

Christine: Well, she interfered with me first. She stole my client.

Manager: She said you stole hers. All the others in the office
confirm that you called her client. They all think you were in the
wrong.

Christine: Well, they don't know what Lara's been doing to me....

The nature of the manager's intervention was to take sides and fuel the fire of anger between Christine and Lara. He tried to determine blame, then placed the blame. His intervention failed to cool down the conflict. Instead it heated things up. It spurred Christine to develop her own blame story to prove that she was right and Lara was wrong. That caused the situation to become even more polarized. In addition, the manager's comments spread the anger to others, so that the war was no longer just between Christine and Lara. He involved their colleagues in the war as well.

A more successful intervention would have been to stay neutral. A peacemaker promotes peace by setting the stage for productive discussion between the warring parties. A peacemaker creates a physical space, a time when both parties are calm, and an atmosphere of hope and reassurance. He or she remains neutral and encourages each person to express what is on his or her mind. A peacemaker carries and expresses the desire for a peaceful resolution and encourages both parties to be thinking along those lines. Blame is not the issue. Promoting understanding between the parties and finding a solution becomes the focus.

This is the role a mediator plays. A mediator facilitates such a discussion between parties and helps the parties explore solutions. A mediator does not act as a judge (determining blame), a lawyer (advocating for one side), or a detective (collecting evidence to prove guilt or innocence). The mediator is there for both parties equally. She or he aids the parties in rediscovering their partnership by helping them understand and appreciate each other.

Mediation is a skill developed through much training and experience. It's always helpful when a trained, skilled mediator is available. However, sometimes that is impossible. Sometimes we call on others to help because we can't find the way out of war alone and we don't have access to a trained mediator. If you are called on to help parties in distress, your best role is to remain as neutral as possible and encourage the parties to find solutions. Avoid gossiping or taking sides. If you feel you can handle it, then offer to be present for them both when they sit down to talk with one another. Do not feel you have to give them advice (which they will probably resist anyway) or fix the situation. Simply speak with the voice of peace and resolution.

If you yourself are caught in a war and do not have access to a trained mediator, then appeal to the bystanders to remain neutral. Ask them to refrain from joining the war. If you ask for help at all, ask for help in encouraging the other party to be willing to stop the war. Be wary of help from people who are taking sides even if they are at that moment taking your side. Loyalties shift, and people who are on your side today might change sides tomorrow. Also, know that accumulating people on your side can have the same impact as accumulating weapons. Doing so promotes the social "arms race" and can lead to all-out war.

It's important to realize, too, that there are times when one needs a friend. Being involved in an interpersonal war can leave a person feeling very isolated. Find your friends and your supporters, but refrain from enlisting them as part of your social army to help you wage war.

7. Stay with the intention to create peace.
Staying committed to the goal of creating peace is sometimes hard. In the face of attack, hurt, destruction, escalation, rage, injury, and more, it's hard to hold the notion of peace in your heart. It's hard to continue to see the other person as a person worthy of respect if they have continually acted toward you in a disrespectful way. We are humans, not gods, and we are just as susceptible to thoughts of hate and revenge as everyone else. We can lose it, too, and sometimes in the face of an intense attack we do lose it.

Nevertheless, know that it is ultimately important to be able to hold on to a desire for creating peace in our lives, even in the face of war. It is important to hold on to the vision that things can be different and that life can return to a state of calm. If we lose the vision, we lose the possibility of creating the vision. If we hold on to the vision, then even if we can't find our way out of whatever war is taking place in our lives at the moment, peace has a chance of returning to us. There may be some route to interpersonal peace that we do not yet know about—some shift in circumstance or climate that can help it come about. Acknowledge that state of unknowing, and believe in peace. Remember the moments of peace in your life, and believe they can return.

In Closing

Life cycles. Conflict is a part of life. Intense conflict is just as much a part of life as peace is. Conflict is an imbalance. Peace is the return to balance. Life is constantly shifting from balance to imbalance and back again. Gain some internal strength to be able to weather the storms, and learn the skills to help you navigate those storms. This book contains some of the skills you will need; the necessary strength for using those skills lies inside of you. Life helps us develop our internal strength, and different people choose different sources of help. Our help can come from friends, loved ones, spiritual beliefs and practices, psychological counseling, or individual self-examination. Many other sources of inspiration and strength exist as well. Learn to use the tools contained in this book and to call on the sources of inspiration and strength in your life. Hold on to the vision of peace, open your heart and mind to the possibility of discovery through other people, and take care of your needs while helping others fulfill theirs—even through the challenges, even in the face of war.

References

Evans, P., *The Verbally Abusive Relationship* (Avon, MA: Adams Media Corporation, 1992).

Fisher, R., and Ury, W., *Getting to Yes* (New York: Penguin Books USA Inc., 1991).

Goleman, D., *Emotional Intelligence* (New York: Bantam Books, 1997).

Hall, E., *The Silent Language* (New York: Anchor Books, 1973).

Inter-Change Consultants, *Skills for Working in a Diverse Environment* (New York: Train the Trainer Program, 1981, 2002).

Jacobson, N., and Gottman, J., *When Men Batter Women* (New York: Simon and Schuster, 1998).

Jayne, P., *Ditch That Jerk* (Alameda, CA: Hunter House, 2000).

Parry, D., *Warriors of the Heart* (Bainbridge Island, WA: Earthstewards Network, 1997).

Raider, E., and Coleman, S., *Collaborative Negotiation Skills* (New York: International Center for Cooperation and Conflict Resolution at Teacher's College, Columbia University, 1992, 1997).

Stone, M., *When God Was a Woman* (New York: Harcourt Brace and Company, 1978).

Wheatley, M., *Turning to One Another* (San Francisco, CA: Berrett-Koehler Publishers, Inc., 2002).

Recommended Reading

ಳಿ

Chopra, D., *The Path to Love* (New York: Harmony Books, 1996).

Cohen, A., *I Had It All the Time* (Haiku, HI: Alan Cohen Publications, 1995).

Hanh, T. N., *Peace Is Every Step* (New York: Bantam Books, 1991).

Tannen, D., *You Just Don't Understand: Women and Men in Conversation* (New York: Ballantine Books, 1990).

Resources

Corporate/Professional

Inter-Change Consultants
Provides dynamic, skills-based training for organizations and individuals. Offices in Atlanta, GA; New York, NY; North Bergen, NJ; and Washington, DC.
Websites: www.interchangeinternational.com
      www.interchangeconsultants.com

Educational

Educators for Social Responsibility
Helps educators throughout the United States create safe, caring, respectful, and productive learning environments. Provides curricula, staff development, and resources for parents, teachers, and students. Located in Cambridge, MA.
Website: www.esrnational.org

Educators for Social Responsibility Metropolitan Area
Provides curricula, staff development, and resources for teachers, parents, and students in the New York City area.
Website: www.esrmetro.org

Operation Respect
Founded by Peter Yarrow of the folk group Peter, Paul and Mary. Provides educational resources and staff development across the United States, designed to reduce behaviors such as ridicule and bullying. Located in New York City.
Website: www.dontlaugh.org

Mediation and Peace Information

Association for Conflict Resolution
A professional organization dedicated to enhancing the practice and public understanding of conflict resolution. You can find family mediators and gain useful information about mediation and conflict resolution at the organization's website.
Website: www.acresolution.org

Justice Center of Atlanta
Works to relieve the emotional, interpersonal, and financial costs of conflict, wherever it occurs, as rapidly as possible. Also provides mediation and training services. Located in Atlanta, GA.
Website: www.justicecenter.org

Index